TENNIS MEDIC

TENNIS MEDIC

CONDITIONING, SPORTS MEDICINE, AND TOTAL FITNESS FOR EVERY PLAYER

STEVEN R. LEVISOHN, M.D.

and

HARVEY B. SIMON, M.D.

Foreword by Stan Smith

Illustrations by Bruce Terizian

THE C.V. MOSBY COMPANY

ST. LOUIS   NEW YORK   TORONTO

For information contact The C.V. Mosby Company
11830 Westline Industrial Drive, St. Louis, Missouri 63146

Library of Congress Cataloging in Publication Data
Levisohn, Steven R.
Tennis medic.

Includes index.
1. Tennis—Accidents and injuries. 2. Tennis—
Physiological aspects. 3. Physical fitness. I. Simon,
Harvey B. (Harvey Bruce), 1942–   . II. Title.
[DNLM: 1. Athletic Injuries. 2. Sports. QT 260 L666t]
RC1220.T4L48   1984   617′.1027   84-14910
ISBN 0-8016-4669-3

M/VH/VH   9 8 7 6 5 4 3 2 1   05/A/607

Printed in the United States of America

Contents

Foreword

As a professional tennis player who has had his share of aches and pains, I have long recognized the importance of conditioning and nutrition for the prevention and treatment of injuries. Not only have I spent a great deal of time seeking the best treatment for certain injuries, but also I have tried diligently to keep from being reinjured and sidelined. Although I am not qualified as a doctor (I do have an honorary degree in Humane Letters), I *have* devoted more time than most to studying my body's "works" to get top performance out of it for my career in tennis.

I also have had many amateur players consult me about a number of the subjects covered in *Tennis Medic*. Usually, I have thought that injured players should find out the answer to their specific problems from a qualified doctor; only a doctor can dispense information sufficiently tailored to a player's individual makeup and needs.

However, Dr. Levisohn and Dr. Simon have covered so many topics comprehensively that this work is a valuable medical tool. Of particular importance is their discussion of how to prevent the most common tennis injuries. Simple and cogent answers are provided to questions such as what to do when certain muscles get just a *little* sore, to keep these aches from becoming major or chronic. Most of us aren't concerned with the symptoms of an injury until the pain gets so bad that it jumps up and grabs us, ultimately landing us on the disabled list. Take it from me: the worst position to be in is to be eager and willing to play but unable to fulfill that desire because of a physical problem; there is no greater frustration for a competitive tennis player.

Particularly worth noting is the section in this book dealing with preparing and playing in sun and heat. There are some very good tips here, as well as a thoughtful presentation of the reasons for measures such as drinking lots of water and protecting your skin. After reading this chapter you may find that you have been treating your body very badly indeed. I know that I made it unnecessarily difficult for myself many times in my career by not guarding against dehydration and sunburn.

There are also many myths about nutrition and general conditioning that are dispelled by some clear explanations by these two doctors. For example, they show how eating a candy bar for instant energy is actually not helpful, but harmful.

Because tennis is such a physically demanding sport, there are many actions you can take to prepare for the game that will significantly improve your performance and improve your results. If your goal is to compete to win, taking a tip or two from these pages will give you a step up on your favorite opponent.

I know that this book will save you some visits to the doctor—and hopefully it will also enable you to reach your potential and become a more effective tennis player. Certainly, if you are aware of how to prevent and handle injuries, you will be able to play longer and enjoy your time both on and off the court. I expect that you will find this to be a useful book.

Stan Smith

Preface

Tennis players are justifiably proud of their sport. No sport requires more individual ability than tennis, and few athletes spend as much time practicing technique, examining equipment, and studying strategy as tennis players.

Unfortunately, tennis players cannot be as proud of the way they take care of their bodies. Although there are exceptions, most players—from the novice to the club player to the pro—spend relatively little time and energy on conditioning and preparation. In our experience the average player understands much more about lobs and smashes than about the aches and pains that affect his own body.

We can understand how this disparity came about. Court time is limited, and so the usual answer to "Tennis anyone?" is to leap to the baseline, fire off a few practice strokes, and move right to the first serve. In addition, because most tennis players train and practice as individuals rather than in teams, they are not exposed to trainers or coaches who can teach conditioning. Finally, we would be the first to admit that tennis is more interesting than tendinitis and playing is more fun than exercising.

Unfortunately, the literature of tennis shares this bias. There are many fine books on technique and strategy but woefully few on conditioning and injuries. *Tennis Medic* is designed to fill this void. We won't try to convert you from tennis to body-building or from *Tennis Magazine* to *The New England Journal of Medicine*, but we will try to show you how conditioning can improve your tennis, prevent injuries, and enhance your health.

Tennis Medic is divided into three sections. Part I deals with conditioning. Our theme is simple: you should get yourself into shape for tennis instead of simply relying on tennis to get you into shape. There are three major aspects of conditioning for tennis, and we have devoted a chapter to each: training for stamina and speed, training for power, and training for range and flexibility. These regimens alone won't enable you to strike fear into the heart of John McEnroe tomorrow; but if you stick with this program, your game will improve, and just as important, you will have fewer injuries.

Even with the most careful conditioning, injuries still occur from time to time. Part II deals with common tennis pains and injuries. We discuss the recognition and treatment of the whole range of tennis ailments, starting with the head and moving all the way to the toes. Some of these problems are tennis classics, such as tennis elbow, tennis leg, and tennis toe; others are less familiar but no less important to you if you happen to be afflicted. Our emphasis is on what you can do for yourself, but we include warning signs that should send you to your doctor for expert help. The unifying theme of this section is the early recognition of problems and the use of simple measures for active rehabilitation and a rapid return to tennis.

Although our focus is tennis, the final section of *Tennis Medic* goes beyond the courts to look at tennis and total fitness. We start out by showing you how you can get your body into shape for tennis; in Part III we show you how tennis can fit into a program of good nutrition and sensible exercise for optimal health.

Tennis Medic won't turn you into a doctor, much less a tennis pro; but we hope that it will help you understand how your body works and how you can help it work best for you on the courts. After all is said and done, our goals are the same: better tennis with fewer injuries.

Since this is a book on tennis medicine, you may be interested in our medical background. We are graduates of Harvard Medical School, where we now serve as faculty members. We both practice medicine at Massachusetts General Hospital and have many athletes among our patients. Dr. Levisohn is President of the Boston Fitness Group, which designs fitness programs for industry. Dr. Simon is a member of Harvard's Cardiovascular Health Center, which uses exercise and nutrition to treat and prevent cardiovascular disease. We are both members of the American College of Sports Medicine and are dedicated amateur athletes.

During the course of these activities we have become interested in reaching beyond our patients and our students to "spread the word" on fitness and health to wider audiences. For the past five years we have written monthly columns and features for *Tennis*

Magazine, where we now serve as contributing editors. Numerous questions from readers and patients have stimulated us to put together this comprehensive program of conditioning, injury management, and total fitness for the tennis player.

Steven R. Levisohn
Harvey B. Simon

Acknowledgments

It is certainly difficult, if not impossible, to single out a few names from among the many who have provided us with encouragement and help during the writing of *Tennis Medic*. Our families have provided continued support and forebearance. Our editors at The C.V. Mosby Company have been invaluable, and over the years the editors of *Tennis Magazine* also have contributed important information and advice.

We are very grateful to Kris Nelson, R.N., for modeling for the illustrations. Our thanks also to Judy Feiner, Debbie Cutliff, Debbi DeSimone, and Nancy LaFarge for their excellent work on the manuscript.

Many colleagues have contributed important information and advice. In particular, we gratefully acknowledge the efforts of Drs. Hugh Chandler, Dinesh Patel, and Don Goldenberg, all of whom reviewed the manuscript in detail.

Steven R. Levisohn
Harvey B. Simon

Conditioning for Tennis: How to Prevent Injuries and Improve Your Game

1 Improving Your Stamina and Speed: Aerobic and Anaerobic Training

Tennis is a wonderful sport for players at all skill levels and an excellent form of exercise. If you play tennis long enough, hard enough, and often enough, the game itself can help keep you fit and healthy. However, you should *not* count on tennis to get you into shape. Planning a balanced conditioning program is the best way to get yourself ready for tennis.

Before you even picked up a tennis racquet, you learned the rules of the game. Before you plan your conditioning program, you should understand something about the theory of fitness. A tennis player's body, like a racing car, requires a well-tuned motor, an ample supply of fuel, good springs and shock absorbers, and tough, durable wheels. The "engine" that makes your tennis machine run is made up of three components: your lungs, heart, and circulatory system. In Chapter 1 we will tell you how to tune the engine by aerobic and anaerobic conditioning.

The "wheels" of tennis are, of course, the muscles of your legs, but the muscles of your arms and the rest of your body are of equal importance. Muscular strength and stamina are essential for winning in tennis, and to build these up, you must condition the specific muscles used in your game. In Chapter 2 we will tell you how to go about this.

The "springs and shock absorbers" are your joints and ligaments, and it is important to get them into shape as well. The key is flexibility, which will improve your reach and range and will also cut down on tennis-related injuries. In Chapter 3 we discuss stretching exercises to enhance your flexibility. Even with the best preventive maintenance, your "wheels" or your "springs and shocks" may develop malfunctions from time to time; in Part II of *Tennis Medic* we will tell you how to repair some of those problems.

The fuel that powers the whole machine comes from your diet and is stored in your muscles and other tissues. The major fuel is sugar. The carbohydrates you eat are digested into glucose, a sugar, which is absorbed into your bloodstream and then deposited in your muscles. For efficient storage the glucose molecules are converted into a compound called *glycogen*. When you need energy to run across court, the glycogen is converted back into glucose, or simple sugar, before it is burned for energy. Both the engine and its fuel supply are very complex and are obviously crucial for both health and sports. Therefore we've devoted Part III of *Tennis Medic* to nutrition (Chapter 15) and the heart (Chapter 16).

First, we'll sketch how the parts of your tennis machine work together so you'll understand how to get them into shape. Your lungs take up oxygen from the air. Oxygen enters the blood, travels to the heart, and is pumped through the circulation to all the tissues of your body. When you exercise, your hard-working muscles need more oxygen, so the lungs breathe faster, the heart pumps harder, and the circulation directs more blood to the muscles. Oxygen moves from the blood into the muscle tissues. At the same time waste products produced during exercise leave the muscles and are carried away by the blood. The major waste product is carbon dioxide, which is exhaled by the lungs to complete this miraculously efficient cycle.

In this simplified outline we have neglected one important element. Your muscles can burn their fuel (glycogen) in one of two ways. If your heart and lungs can deliver enough oxygen, your muscles will use oxygen to burn the glycogen up completely. This is the most efficient way to generate energy and is called *aerobic metabolism*. But if your muscles are working all out, they will need more energy than they can get aerobically. At full power your muscles use up all the oxygen your heart, lungs, and circulation can deliver, so they have to burn glycogen without oxygen. This is called *anaerobic metabolism*, and it is less efficient because it generates less energy but more waste products.

The point at which your muscles switch from aerobic to anaerobic metabolism is called the *anaerobic threshold*. Even if you forget all this terminology, you'll always recognize the anaerobic threshold because you'll suddenly start to breathe faster and harder. If you keep pushing yourself beyond the threshold, you'll feel short of breath and your muscles will develop pain and fatigue. Ultimately you'll run out of gas.

How does all this relate to conditioning? The answer is simple: conditioning can make the whole machine run better, faster, and longer. Two kinds of conditioning are important. *Endurance training* will build up your aerobic capacity. Your heart will be able to pump more oxygen, your circulation will deliver it to your muscles more efficiently, and your muscles will improve their ability to use the oxygen to generate energy. In a sense, your gas mileage will improve: endurance training builds *stamina*.

However, as Bjorn Borg has pointed out, tennis is not a marathon but rather an extended series—like 100 or more—of 10-yard dashes. In addition to stamina, you need speed, which can be developed through *speed training*. Your anaerobic threshold will increase, and your muscles will improve their ability to function even after you have crossed the threshold.

By now you are probably ready to get out of the classroom and onto the court. But don't skip the rest of this chapter: a balanced fitness program *will* help your game.

Winning tennis requires a subtle mix of skills. Technique and strategy are obvious requirements, and the honing of these skills seems best achieved by working personally with a teaching pro. The strength and flexibility essential to execute those moves require conditioning, as outlined in the next two chapters. Although skill and strength are necessary for winning tennis, they are not enough. Many a match has been lost in the fourth or fifth set because of fatigue. You may not even be aware that this is happening because the excitement of the match may prevent you from recognizing that you are tired. As you begin to run out of energy, you will lose half a step in getting to the ball. If you are out of position, your strokes will suffer and you will begin to lose points. Fatigue has its mental aspects, too: when you reach the limits of your physical endurance, your competitive urge and winning instincts begin to suffer.

The combination of fatigue, slowness, and discouragement spells defeat. How can you avoid these pitfalls? The answer is conditioning.

Tennis, of course, is fun. Training and conditioning are work, but work that will pay off in extending your pleasure in the game itself. Building your endurance and speed will greatly improve your game. In addition, conditioning helps cut down significantly on tennis-related injuries. Finally, a conditioning program can be pursued year round so that you can stay fit even off-season, when your court time may be limited.

Endurance Training

Horse trainers call it "foundation," runners call it a "base," and baseball players call it "legs." On the tennis circuit it is generally called "wind." Whatever you call it, it's the ability to play hard and fast, to recover from strenuous exertion quickly, and to get moving again for a long afternoon match. In medical terms, it's *aerobic power.*

Aerobic or endurance exercises are those in which large muscle groups are used in a rhythmic, repetitive fashion for prolonged periods. Examples of aerobic activities are brisk walking, jogging, swimming, bicycling, cross-country skiing, and aerobic dancing. The majority of time you spend on a tennis court will also involve aerobic exercise. In aerobics the heart rate is raised substantially but never reaches its maximum level. Because this type of exercise increases the efficiency of the heart, lungs, and circulation, it should be the cornerstone of your tennis conditioning program.

Warm-up

The first step in aerobic conditioning is a warm-up, which is extremely important for two reasons. First, your muscles will loosen up and get warm. Cold, tight muscles are prone to injuries such as muscle pulls and cramps, but the warm-up will help prevent injuries by making your muscles more elastic. A second reason for warming up gradually is to protect your most important muscle—your heart. A warm-up period will give your heart a chance to get into high gear gradually with steady increases in your heart rate and in your cardiac output (the amount of blood pumped by your heart to your tissues). There are many ways to warm up, ranging from brisk walking to practicing your ground strokes, but we would suggest incorporating stretching exercises and gentle calisthenics as outlined in Chapter 3. Five to ten minutes of stretching will increase your flexibility while you warm up your heart and other muscles.

Aerobic Training

After you are warmed up, what's next? Your aerobic conditioning program has to take three elements into account: the *intensity, duration,* and *frequency* of the exercise itself. In terms of *frequency,* it takes three or four workouts per week to really get into shape. If you are playing tennis regularly, you can count an hour of intense singles as an aerobic workout. If you play three or four hard matches per week, you may find that tennis alone will enable you to maintain a reasonably good level of aerobic fitness. But the paradox is that competitors who play at this high level are just those who will benefit from even more conditioning. In the last analysis, the frequency of your aerobic workouts will depend on your baseline level of fitness and your personal goals. If you are just getting into shape in the off-season, you should start gradually. It can take muscles 24 to 48 hours to recover from a strenuous workout, so we suggest an every-other-day schedule to ease your body into shape. You should use the off-day to stretch and do calisthenics. As you get into shape, you can increase your workouts to 5 or even 7 days a week. Most people prefer to reserve conditioning workouts for days on which they don't play tennis, but the real enthusiast may even want to do a little running in the evening after a match.

The *duration* of each exercise session will also increase as you get into shape. To start, you should aim for 10 to 15 minutes of aerobic work in addition to your 5- to 10-minute warm-up. If you are out of shape, you will probably have to include some low-intensity exercise in the 10-minute aerobic exercise period; alternating brisk walking with jogging is an example of this. As you improve, you should decrease the amount of lower-level work until you can sustain the full 15 minutes of aerobics. Having built this base, you should gradually extend each exercise period, perhaps aiming to lengthen it by 10% each week until you can sustain aerobic work for 30 minutes of uninterrupted activity. This 30-minute period will provide ideal endurance training for tennis.

If your goal is high-quality, competitive tennis, you may want to extend these levels even further. Even though tennis will remain your favorite sport, you may actually enjoy jogging, biking, rowing, or swimming in their own rights. Remember that the rules stay the same for the accomplished athlete as they are for the novice: you should continue to warm-up slowly, stretch regularly, and increase your work load gradually. Try also to alternate hard days and easy days so that your muscles will have a chance to recover in between workouts.

It's easy to gauge the frequency of your exercise by the calendar and the duration of your aerobics by the clock, but how do you measure *intensity*? This is the most difficult to measure but also the most important element in your tennis conditioning program. There are two simple ways to monitor the intensity of exercise: measuring the heart rate and measuring the respiratory rate. The latter can be estimated quite easily. When you cross the anaerobic threshold, your muscles develop an oxygen debt and build up acid. The increased acid production in turn leads to an increased carbon dioxide production. To get rid of the carbon dioxide, you have to breathe more rapidly. All this may sound complicated, but it's simple for your body and is entirely automatic. You will know when you cross the anaerobic threshold because you will suddenly find yourself breathing rapidly and you will feel breathless or winded. You can be sure you are in the aerobic range by preventing this: work hard enough to break into sweat but not hard enough to feel short of breath. Use the "talking pace" as a guide: if you are exercising aerobically, you should have enough wind in reserve to carry on at least a limited conversation with a companion.

The talking pace rule will prevent you from becoming deprived of oxygen, but you may well err on the side of too much talking and not enough working—in other words, you may not push yourself hard enough to get the full benefits of aerobic exercise. Because of this, heart rate is a much more precise guide to endurance training. You need to do three things to use your heart as a guide to the intensity of exercise:

1. **Learn to take your pulse.** Each heartbeat pumps blood through the arteries, and thus the pulse rate equals the heart rate. The pulse is easiest to feel in the radial artery on the "thumb side" of your wrist or in the carotid artery in your neck, just below and in front of your jaw. Figure 1-1 shows you how to feel these pulses. Practice until you can feel and count the pulse easily at rest. Then practice taking your pulse immediately after exercise, which will be a bit harder since your heart is beating faster. It is important to take the pulse immediately after you stop exercising because your heart rate slows down when you rest. Use a watch with a second hand to count your pulse for 10 seconds, and then multiply by six to get your heart rate per minute. Most people can learn to count their pulse quite accurately, but if you find it difficult, you may want to look into a portable pulse meter. A number of these gadgets are available that are portable, accurate, cute—and expensive.

2. **Know your maximum heart rate.** If you have had an exercise electrocardiogram test (stress test), your maximum heart rate has been measured on a treadmill or bike, so your doctor can tell you the number (see Chapter 15 for a discussion of exercise tests). But if you

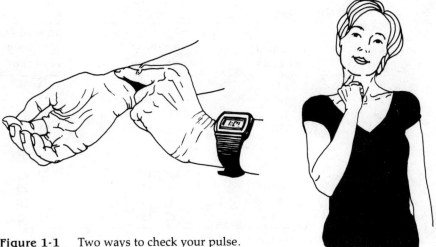

Figure 1-1   Two ways to check your pulse.

haven't had a stress test, you can estimate your predicted maximum heart rate based on your age: just subtract your age in years from 220 to obtain your approximate maximum rate.

3. **Know your target heart rate.** Remember that the idea of aerobics is to work hard, but not all out. This translates to a target heart rate of 70% to 85% of your maximum rate. If you are out of shape or in an older age group, you should initially aim for the lower end of your target heart rate range; if you are young and athletic, you can push toward 85% of your maximum rate.

Your goal should be to keep your heart rate in this target range during your entire aerobic exercise. To help you determine your target range, Table 1-1 shows your target range in beats per minute and in counts per 10-second period. We can give you these targets, but you have to do the exercise yourself. As you get into shape, you will discover a remarkable change in how well you do. Your target range will remain the same, but you will find yourself working much more intensely to stay on target, and as your work capacity increases, your endurance, or wind, on the tennis court will improve as well.

Cool-down

The third part of each aerobic training session is the cool-down. After you've warmed up and worked out, it's very tempting to head straight for the showers. Don't give in to this temptation. Instead, spend 5 to 10 minutes cooling down. These extra few minutes are

Table 1-1   Your target heart rate

Age	Maximum Heart Rate	Target Range Low*	Target Range High†	10-Second Pulse Count Low	10-Second Pulse Count High
20	200	140	170	23	28
25	197	137	166	23	28
30	194	136	165	22	27
35	188	132	160	22	26
40	182	128	155	21	26
45	176	124	150	20	25
50	171	119	145	20	24
55	165	115	140	19	23
60	159	111	135	18	23
65	153	107	130	17	22

*Seventy percent of maximum.
†Eighty-five percent of maximum.

very worthwhile: if you are overheated, your body temperature will return to normal gradually; your heart will be able to gear down steadily; your circulation will have a chance to pump waste products away from your muscles; and your muscles will be able to stretch out and thus escape excessive fatigue, soreness, tightness, and cramps. Slow jogging or walking is good for your cooling down, and because your muscles and ligaments are already warm and supple, stretching exercises are particularly desirable during the cool-down period.

Warnings and Precautions

Before you actually begin your aerobic training program for tennis, a word of caution is in order. If you stay within your target range, you should not have any problems. But you should know certain warning signs that signal you to stop exercising and to check with your doctor. Chest pressure or pain, excessively rapid or irregular heartbeats, extreme shortness of breath or wheezing, light-headedness, undue fatigue or weakness, excessive pallor or sweating, and extreme nausea are among these warning signs. Any of these symptoms may suggest heart trouble. Although endurance training is actually good for your heart, you do have to be alert for potential adverse effects, and it is always a good idea to get a medical checkup before you begin a strenuous training program. The effects of tennis on your heart and circulation are discussed in detail in Chapter 16.

Other less serious signs to watch for as you begin training are excessive or persistent aches in your back, knees, or legs. These musculoskeletal complaints usually mean that you are doing too much, too fast, without enough stretching and warming up. Although most people do experience minor aches and pains en route to fitness, serious problems are uncommon. Go right ahead with your exercise training, remembering only to keep one ear cocked to listen to the signals of your own body.

What Exercises Are Best for You?

What types of aerobic exercise are best to supplement tennis? As we mentioned earlier, tennis itself is reasonable aerobic conditioning, but to bring your aerobic power to its maximum, you would have to play vigorous singles almost every day. In general, we recommend supplementary aerobic training for all serious tennis players. This applies to the beginning or intermediate player who is trying to get into shape for tennis and also to the advanced or competitive player who needs to build extra stamina for winning. Although any aerobic exercise will help your training, some activities are more efficient than others. Table 1-2 compares the approximate energy levels required for racquet sports and other common types of exercise. You can translate these figures into daily terms by remembering that you will get about the same benefits from ¼ mile of swimming, 1 mile of jogging, 5 to 10 minutes of jumping rope, or 3 to 5 miles of bicycling.

Your choice of exercise will depend on what you like, what facilities are available, and the climate in which you live. Many players find that a mix of aerobic exercises is the best answer. Each activity has its particular advantages. For example, running and biking are excellent to build up your legs, which are crucial in tennis. Jumping rope will also strengthen your legs while at the same time helping your speed and coordination. Swimming is excellent conditioning for the whole body, including your arms; because the water instead of your legs supports your weight, swimming is easier on your muscles and joints.

For most players, however, running is the most convenient and efficient aerobic supplement to tennis. If you're just getting started in tennis and you're out of shape, you may have to begin by alternating jogging with brisk walking. For example, you might try walking for 1 to 2 minutes, jogging for 1 to 2 minutes, and then returning to walking. You can repeat this cycle 10 to 12 times on each training day. As you improve, cut down on the amount of walking and increase the amount of jogging, so that you can eventually

Table 1-2   Energy output during tennis in comparison to other activities

Activity	Energy Output (Calories / Hour)*
Racquet sports	
Table tennis	300
Badminton	300
Doubles tennis	300
Singles tennis	420
Squash, paddleball	480
Walking or running	
Strolling 1 mile/hour	120
Level walking 2 miles/hour	150
Level walking 3 miles/hour	240
Brisk walking 4 miles/hour	360
Jogging 5 miles/hour	480
Jogging 6 miles/hour	660
Running 7 miles/hour	760
Bicycling	
6 miles/hour	240
10 miles/hour	360
12 miles/hour	480
Other activities	
Bowling	240
Golf—pulling cart	240
Golf—carrying clubs	300
Calisthenics	300
Ballet	300
Downhill skiing	480
Cross-country skiing	660
Daily living	
Resting	60
Desk work	90
Standing	120
Light housework (dusting, etc.)	150
Heavy housework (vacuuming, etc.)	250
Scrubbing floors	300
Raking leaves	300
Average sexual activity	300

*NOTE: Values are approximate levels for people of average size. Levels of above 300 calories/hour will generally provide aerobic conditioning if the activity is sustained for 20 minutes or longer. Higher energy levels will provide better conditioning. Your work intensity should allow you to attain and sustain (but not exceed) your target heart rate.

sustain a slow run for 15 to 20 minutes. Then gradually increase the time you spend running, so that eventually you can go for 30 to 40 minutes without interruption. Most players will be able to cover 4 to 5 miles in this period, but the time you spend running is really more important than the distance you travel. Remember that you can use your target heart rate to guide your pace, and as you become more fit, you will be able to go further in your allotted time. Obviously, if you are fit to begin with, you can begin your aerobic conditioning at a higher level. But your eventual goal can remain the same, since 4 to 5 miles of running will provide excellent aerobic conditioning. Although some competitive players run every day, it is probably best for most of us to save our longer runs for days on which we don't have hard tennis matches. It's always a good idea to alternate easier workouts with more demanding sessions. But whatever mix you choose, we recommend that you work out aerobically 3 or 4 times per week. This is especially important to maintain your fitness in the off-season, when you may have less court time available.

Speed Training

For the tennis player, even the most exhausting five-set match is fun. On the other hand, jogging and other forms of endurance training are work. Training is a means to an end, and it's worth putting in the miles chiefly because your tennis game will improve. But if endurance training is work, speed training is torture. Why do it? Because tennis requires bursts of great speed as well as stamina or endurance.

The idea behind speed training is based on the distinction between aerobic and anaerobic exercise. *Aerobic* exercise doesn't build up an oxygen debt because your heart and circulation supply oxygen at the same rate that your muscles need it. Thus you are limited only by how good a pump your heart is and how much endurance your muscles have. In contrast, *anaerobic* exercise means your muscles are working so hard that they outstrip their oxygen supply. This has two consequences. First, your muscles have to burn fuel (glycogen) incompletely and inefficiently when they are anaerobic—in fact, muscles get only a twentieth the energy from the same amount of fuel when they are anaerobic. Second, waste products such as lactic acid build up, and this causes fatigue, cramps, and ultimately pain.

To be blunt, speed training can be painful. But if you condition your muscles with anaerobic training, they will be able to function much more efficiently under these adverse circumstances. As a result, you will have the extra reserves of speed you need to charge the net for a drive or sprint back to the baseline to retrieve a lob.

Speed training goes by many names. The physiologist refers to it as anaerobic conditioning, and coaches often speak of it as interval running or repeats. Many players call these workouts wind sprints. But by any name, speed training adds up to just one thing: hard work. The idea is to push your body close to its limits not just once, but again and again.

Obviously you run the risk of serious injury if you interpret this to be nothing more than running full speed until you drop and then scraping yourself off the court to do it over and over again. Proper speed work requires a carefully thought out, tightly controlled plan. It also means you have to be in good shape both aerobically and in terms of your muscles and joints before you even get started. Finally, speed work requires a subtle mix of determination to push yourself to the point of pain and the common sense to say enough is enough.

Sprinting is the best way to build up your speed for tennis. To avoid injuries, limit your speed drills to no more than two per week. Always begin with stretching and then jogging so that your muscles are warm, your joints are loose, and your heart is geared up gradually before you stress yourself fully. Once you are warmed up, you can start sprinting. This does *not* mean a mad 100-yard dash followed by an inglorious collapse to the ground. Instead, you should have a clear plan and a disciplined sense of pace. Your muscles become anaerobic at about 90% of their maximum effort, so we suggest that you try to run at about 90% of your maximum instead of all out. At first you can aim for 10 to 20 seconds of sprinting. When you have finished, don't come to an abrupt stop. Instead, walk or jog during the recovery period. As a rule of thumb, it is reasonable to allow two or three times as much time for recovery; thus, if you sprint for 20 seconds, walk or jog for 40 to 60 seconds. You won't feel rested and fresh after this recovery period, but your heart rate will be lower and you will be ready to sprint again. Try another 10 to 20 seconds of sprinting followed by a recovery period of 20 to 60 seconds. Repeat this cycle three to six times, depending on how hard you're working and what kind of shape you're in. Above all, remember to walk or jog after you conclude your workout to give yourself a cool-down period. Finally, thorough stretching is an excellent way to terminate your speed workout.

As you improve, you can increase the number of sprints, increase your speed, lengthen the distance you sprint, or shorten the recovery period. However, remember that you are not training for track but for tennis; concentrate on rapid acceleration and short bursts of speed rather than on ¼-mile intervals. Most important, don't go overboard. You've got to push yourself hard for successful speed training, but you must be equally careful not to overdo it; determination and drive must be counterbalanced by discipline and common sense.

Although we heartily recommend endurance training for all tennis players, we must admit that speed training is not for everyone. The weekend doubles player is likely to do more harm than good with this type of training. But for serious competitive or club-level players, interval training can help build speed and result in winning tennis.

Remember that interval work is a tool to improve tennis, not an end in itself. Don't get carried away. Limit your speed drills to one or two sessions per week. Don't do wind sprints if you are injured, sick, or overly tired. Don't put yourself through hard speed workouts within 48 hours of an important tennis match.

We stress these precautions because speed work can lead to injuries. However, if you follow these precautions and listen to the signals of your body, interval training can be an excellent conditioning tool. In combination with aerobics, strength work, and stretching, speed training can help get your body in shape for top-flight tennis.

2 Improving Your Power: Conditioning to Build Strength for Tennis

Nothing replaces natural talent. Some of us are genetically endowed with superb timing, coordination, and court sense. The rest of us have to make up, by conditioning, for what our grandparents failed to provide. In the preceding chapter we discussed the importance of aerobic conditioning to strengthen your heart. In these next two chapters we will discuss the other aspects of conditioning—the way your muscles can be made to work best for you.

Goals

The goals of muscular conditioning are to develop your strength, endurance, and flexibility. These factors will improve your ability to hit the ball when you want to, where you want to, with adequate power, and with the reach and range of motion essential for you to control your game. When you are in shape, you'll be able to keep all this up for a full match, and, of equal importance, you'll be able to play again the next day—free of injuries.

However, like cardiovascular endurance, muscular strength and flexibility are physical attributes that you have to work to maintain, especially as you get beyond the age of 30. Also like cardiovascular endurance, age is no barrier, and these skills can be maintained even into the 70s and 80s. In fact, tennis "super seniors" who have been tested showed significantly less adverse effects of aging in terms of endurance, strength, speed, and coordination when compared with their sedentary friends.

The corollary of all this has to do with injuries. Most nontraumatic tennis injuries are due to overuse, that is, doing more than you should at your current level of skill or conditioning. Whether it is "tennis elbow," "tennis leg," back sprain, bad knees, or shoulder pain, most tennis injuries are preventable by a proper combination of muscular conditioning and flexibility.

For most of us, the lesson is "get in shape to play tennis; don't depend on tennis to get you in shape." If you do get into shape, you will play better, longer, and with fewer injuries.

The Equipment: Muscles, Tendons, and Joints

We discussed your cardiorespiratory system—the pump, the tubing, and the oxygen-exchange equipment—in Chapter 1. Before discussing how to improve the rest of the equipment, let's review what it is, how it works, and how it is influenced by conditioning.

Muscles

Muscles are specialized tissues with the ability to contract and shorten. Voluntary, or skeletal, muscles always bridge a joint, providing the power to bend a joint (flexion) or straighten it (extension). Muscles develop *strength* and *power* in direct relation to their activity. If unused, they weaken. If used, they increase in strength. Muscles also develop *endurance* in relation to conditioning. If they are exercised repetitively against low resistance, endurance improves, probably because of the development of larger intracellular stores of energy-containing sugars, or carbohydrates, stored as a lightly compacted polymer called *glycogen*. However, strength and conditioning are *specific*. If you pedal a bicycle with only one leg, as experiments have shown, that leg, but *not* the other, will develop strength and endurance. If you practice only your backhand, it will not improve your service.

Tendons

Muscles are attached to bones via *tendons*, fibrous tissues that you notice most when they are overused and you get tendinitis. Tendons also respond to conditioning by becoming stronger but are otherwise inert and do not contribute actively to exercise. Most tendons are covered by sheaths and are cushioned by *bursal sacs* as they run over bony prominences. Bursas produce lubrication for tendon motion but can also be affected by overuse and wear and tear. Although your body has dozens of bursas, you won't hear from any of them until you are injured; then the pain and stiffness of *bursitis* will quickly underline the importance of these small structures.

Joints

Joints are complex structures and are discussed specifically later when we talk about injuries. Joints are composed of bones and their cartilaginous surfaces, which are surrounded by a joint capsule containing lubricating fluid. As noted earlier, muscles pass across joints and are vital to the motion of joints, and in many ways the muscles also provide protection and some stability for joints. Stability is primarily provided by *ligaments*—bands of fibrous tissue similar to tendons that encase joints to limit joint motions to their proper range. The key joints used in tennis are ankles, knees, the lower back (which involves many joints), elbows, and shoulders, although all joints (including, it seems, the jaw) are involved to some degree.

Conditioning affects joints in two ways. First, their function, integrity, and resistance to injury depend in large measure on the strength of the muscles surrounding them. Second, your ability to play well depends on the joint's ability to function through its entire physiologic range of motion. If you can't straighten out (extend) your elbow completely because of poor flexibility, your shots will suffer and you will develop tennis elbow. Similarly, if your shoulder is stiff, your service will be affected.

Principles of Conditioning

When we discuss muscular conditioning and how it affects you, we are really discussing the principles underlying the development of flexibility, strength, and endurance.

Flexibility

Flexibility is a major factor in controlling muscle function. Since muscles are arranged in competing groups around joints—one group extending, the other group flexing—poor muscular flexibility will make the opposing group work harder and can be a major cause of injuries. Thus in any modern discussion of conditioning, flexibility plays a big role. Although you may think of flexibility or inflexibility in terms of joint motion, it actually depends primarily on your muscles and tendons and to some extent on the joint ligament and capsule. During games, if your muscles are tight, when you suddenly stretch them reaching for a shot, you run the risk of straining or rupturing the muscle or causing tendinitis. Flexibility enhances your reach and your game and prevents injuries. We will discuss flexibility and stretching exercises in detail in Chapter 3.

Muscular Strength and Endurance

In virtually all sports, the stronger you are, the better you will play. The difference in strength is probably the major cause of the difference in performance between women and men, whether in tennis, swimming, running, of even golfing. You rarely need all the strength you can muster, but your unused reserve of strength is still important. For example, if you are twice as strong, you can achieve a given output using 30% of your maximum strength, rather than 60%. This affects the rate at which you use up energy and your control, timing, and endurance.

Any discussion of muscular conditioning is generally divided into *strength, endurance* (the number of repetitions of any particular motion), and *specificity* (the requirement to exercise a particular muscle group to strengthen it: what you train improves, and what you don't weakens).

Strength conditioning involves exerting force against resistance. That resistance can be provided in many ways; for example, an immovable object provides a fixed resistance. Pushing against it constitutes an *isometric* exercise; no motion occurs, but muscle tension increases so that conditioning occurs. This type of exercise is often beneficial in rehabilitation from a injury in which joint motion may be harmful but strength should be improved.

At the other end of the spectrum, low-resistance exercise may be achieved by using a light dumbbell or doing calisthenics. These exercises can be repeated many times before the point of fatigue. This is called *isotonic* exercise; muscles contract or shorten without greatly increasing their tension. For most sports, isotonic conditioning is preferable, since muscle action takes place through a full range of motion.

Obviously, isotonics and isometrics are not pure entities but actually lie on a continuum. At the one end isometrics represent the extreme example of high-resistance exercise, which is usually anaerobic, maximum work of short duration. At the other end of the spectrum, isotonic exercise is usually low-resistance, aerobic, sub-maximum, and repetitive exercise of longer duration. Maximum muscular *strength* develops through high-resistance, low-repetition exercise (for example, a set of 6 to 10 repetitions). In contrast, maximum muscular *endurance* is built through low-resistance, high-repetition work. For men, increased muscular bulk also develops from high-resistance exercise. Women, on the other hand, will not develop bulk with exercise, since they lack the male hormone responsible for muscular hypertrophy, testosterone. This should be stressed, since the myth about bulky muscles has kept many women from working with weights. On the other hand, increased muscular tone will firm you up and improve the appearance of both men and women.

In general, we recommend a combined approach. Your weight work can be tilted toward high-resistance, low-repetition exercises for strength. You can rely on calisthenics, endurance sports, and practice strokes to develop muscular endurance. This approach will provide both stroking power and staying power.

Resistance Training and Weight Lifting

Resistance work can be done either with free weights or with exercise machines, such as the Universal Gym, Nautilus, or Cam II. These machines work through a series of cams, pulleys and levers, or hydraulics to provide resistance to motion. They are designed to be very specific in terms of the muscle groups affected. Although they sound complicated, once you learn to use a machine, it is actually easier than free weights. Since "one size fits all," exercise machines have disadvantages if you happen to be too weak, short, long, etc. They are also subject to intense promotion, usually on unsubstantiated grounds. Many tennis clubs have purchased them but, unfortunately, don't provide anyone to teach their proper use, and so they sit in splendid isolation. We will outline some of the common exercises with both free weights and Nautilus and Universal Gym equipment, but nothing replaces good hands-on instruction with a skilled coach or teacher.

General Guidelines for Resistance Training

Intensity. To begin strength work, you should pick a resistance or weight that is approximately 60% of what you can achieve with a single maximum effort. A weight of this amount should allow you to do about 6 to 10 repetitions.

Sets. Exercises should be done in sets. If you select a realistic resistance weight, a set should consist of about 6 to 10 repetitions of the exercise. If you can't do at least six repetitions, decrease the resistance. If you can do more than 10, increase the resistance—but as a rule, increase it by no more than 10%. During each exercise session you should do each set one to three times. Remember that your objective is tennis, not body-building. Don't go overboard: stick to simple, proven patterns.

Frequency. Done properly, weight training is tiring, and your muscles need time to recover. You can benefit from doing it as little as once per week, but under no circumstances should you do strength training more often than three times per week without a knowledgeable coach helping you.

Muscular work is done during both the contraction and the relaxation phases of resistance training. In general, the relaxation phase should be done more slowly than the contraction phase, with a brief pause between each phase.

Specific Exercises for Strength and Endurance

In the following pages we will give specific advice to strengthen some of the key areas of your body. For each of these there are a number of different types of exercise. Some are recreational (such as biking, running, or doing calisthenics); some are just plain work (like weight or resistance training). The former will provide more muscular endurance; the latter will provide more muscular power. Strength and resistance training is further subdivided into free weights and Universal Gym or Nautilus regimens. What you do will depend in part on factors such as your assessment of your own needs, the availability of equipment, time constraints, and your goals. At the end of this section we provide a model program for both the casual weekend player with limited time and the high-intensity player.

The Legs

A tennis player travels on his legs, so let's start with individual programs for the lower extremities. Running is the best way to condition your legs. As noted earlier, distance running will condition your heart more than sprints will. Jogging will also provide the foundation for the muscular endurance you need to play a full five sets without letting down. It will also build up the circulatory response you need to recover quickly and get rid of metabolic waste products. So that is the first exercise: run. Run every chance you get, at least 5 miles a week. Run easily, at a slow pace. Run to warm up. Get your legs used to running.

Actually, running is not a single exercise but is really two types of exercise. Jogging primarily requires the use of hamstring muscles. In sprinting you use the quadriceps muscles at the front of the thigh and the calf muscles. Remember "specificity": you have to exercise the muscles you'll be using. Tennis is a series of short sprints, but a five-set match requires endurance as well. Therefore you should

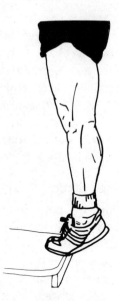

Figure 2-1
Calf raises. Stand with your toes on
a 2-inch block, heels on the floor, and
raise yourself until you are standing
on your toes and the balls of your
feet. Then lower yourself slowly
to the ground.

build both sprinting and jogging into your conditioning program.

Lower extremity resistance training also will increase your speed and your power. Remember that tennis requires quick starts, quick stops, and quick changes of direction. Begin with your calves. Here, exercises with free weights are simpler and better than what you can do with the various machines. Two examples are illustrated. In the first exercise stand with your toes on a board, heels on the floor, and raise yourself (Figure 2-1). Build up to 20 to 30 repetitions. The exercise can be made more difficult by carrying dumbbells in your hands and eventually by doing one leg independently of the other. Start with a 5-pound dumbbell in each hand or a 10-pound barbell and work up.

The second exercise puts more stress on the soleus muscle and the upper portion of the calf, muscles that are prone to injury in tennis. This exercise is done while sitting (Figure 2-2). By bending your knees, you tend to isolate the soleus and upper calf muscles and exercise them selectively. Start with a barbell of about 10 pounds. Rest the barbell on a pad across your knees, and again work up to 20 to 30 repetitions before increasing the weight. The importance of this exercise is obvious when you think of the number of situations in tennis when you start or stop suddenly with your knees bent.

The next set of exercises involves the muscles of the knees and thighs. As noted, sprinting and running up hills or stairs strengthen

Figure 2-2
Sitting toe-ups for soleus muscle and upper calves. Sit on a bench with a 10-pound barbell resting on a pad on your knees. Slowly raise your knees up, and then return them to the starting position.

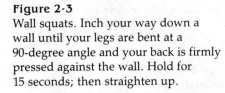

Figure 2-3
Wall squats. Inch your way down a wall until your legs are bent at a 90-degree angle and your back is firmly pressed against the wall. Hold for 15 seconds; then straighten up.

Figure 2-4   Squats. Stand with your feet parallel, about shoulder width apart, with a barbell carrying 10 to 20 pounds across your shoulders. Grasp the bar as shown. Bend your knees until your thighs are parallel to the floor, but no further! Return to an upright position. Repeat 6 to 10 times. Do not bounce.

the anterior thigh muscles (the quadriceps), which are responsible for the integrity of the knee. Another enjoyable exercise that will strengthen the quadriceps and the knee is bicycling. These activities enhance muscular endurance and give your legs and knees the staying power you need.

For increased knee strength (and decreased chances of injury), higher-resistance exercises are necessary. The simplest are partial knee-bends, which are part of any good calisthenics regimen. But avoid *deep* knee-bends lower than 90 degrees, since they can cause torn knee cartilage. Build up to the point where you can do 20 to 30 partial knee-bends. This exercise is particularly important for women, who often have weaker quadriceps than men. If you find that

Figure 2-5   Leg extension. Adjust the weight stack for your level. Begin with 10 to 20
pounds. Sit on the edge of the leg-extension machine, and hook the tops
of your feet under the rollers. Grab the bench for support, and slowly
extend your legs fully until your knees lock. Hold for the count of 1,
then slowly return to the starting position. Repeat 6 to 10 times. Be careful
if it causes pain or grinding noises over the knee caps.

knee-bends are painful, your muscles are underdeveloped. To
correct this, start with the following isometric exercise: squat with
your shoulders and back against a wall (again avoiding bending
your knees past a 90-degree angle), and hold this posture for
gradually increasing times (Figure 2-3). You'll be surprised at how
hard this is at first. Eventually you should be able to hold this
posture for 2 to 3 minutes. Then go on to more dynamic exercises,
such as partial knee-bends, when you have developed adequate
strength.

Knee-bends can be the basis for weight training exercises as well.
As shown in Figure 2-4, do partial knee-bends (called squats) with
a barbell supported on your shoulders. Squat less than half way

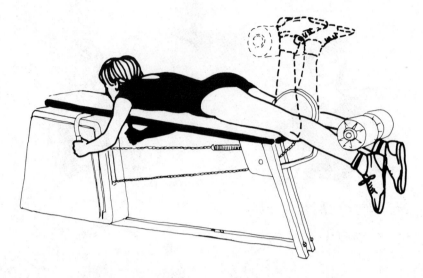

Figure 2-6   Leg curls for the hamstring muscles. Adjust the weight, beginning with 10 to 20 pounds. Lie face down on the bench, hooking your heels under the rollers. Grab the handles, and slowly bend your legs as far as possible. Hold for a count of 1, then lower to starting position. Repeat 6 to 10 times.

and straighten up, repeating this up to 10 times for a set. When you can do two full sets of 10, add 5% to 10% more weight.

Exercise machines make this type of exercise very easy and, in addition, allow you to work the upper thigh muscles and hamstrings. Universal Gym and Nautilus offer similar devices for the lower extremities. Quadriceps are strengthened on a *leg extension* machine (Figure 2-5). Fully extend your legs until your knees lock, hold for a count of 1, and lower to starting position. *Leg curls* work the hamstring muscles with some secondary help for calves and buttocks (Figure 2-6).

This set of exercises provides a good regimen for forward and backward movements of your upper leg. However, two groups of muscles often used in tennis are those which abduct the leg (move the leg away from the midline) or adduct the leg (move the leg toward the midline). These muscles are responsible for side-to-side motion. Equipment to build these muscles is hard to find, but since lateral motion in tennis relies on the integrity of these muscles, and since painful injuries such as groin pulls await us if we neglect them, it is very worthwhile to develop a program for yourself. Endurance for these muscles is increased by doing jumping jacks (Figure 2-7).

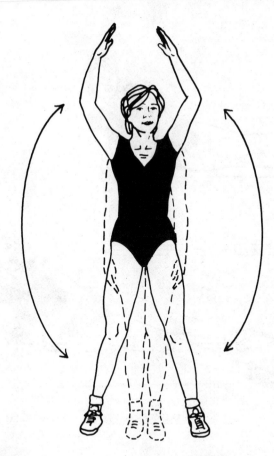

Figure 2-7   Jumping jacks. Simply jump and spread your legs while raising your hands above your head. Then jump and return to the start. Begin with 10 and build up to 50.

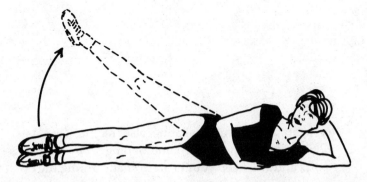

Figure 2-8   Abduction exercises are done while lying on a floor and raising your leg with the knee straight as far as possible. Turn slightly so that you face the floor and exercise the muscles to the back of your leg and buttocks. Then slowly lower to the floor. Do 5 to 6 times initially and build up to 20 to 30.

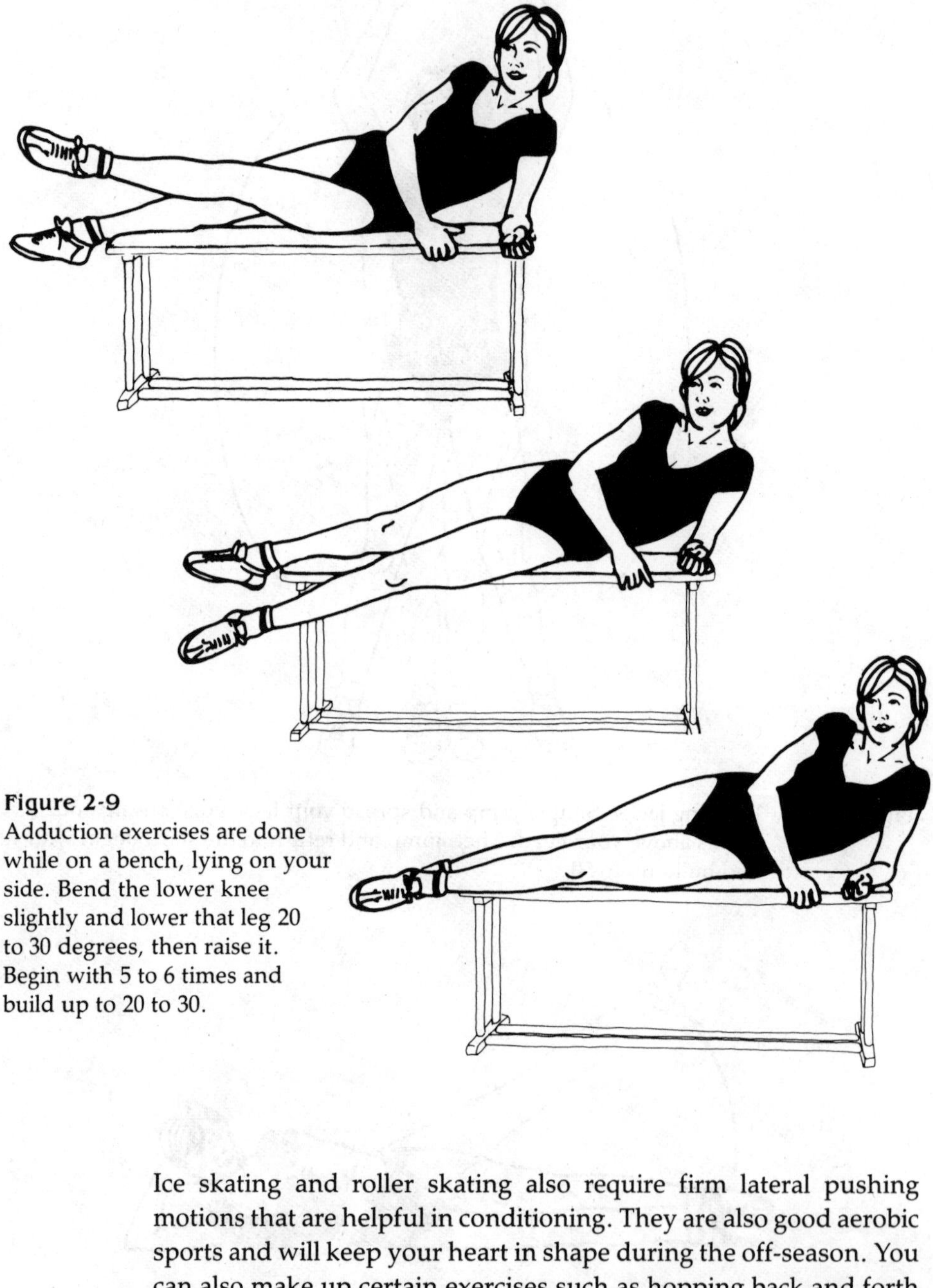

Figure 2-9
Adduction exercises are done
while on a bench, lying on your
side. Bend the lower knee
slightly and lower that leg 20
to 30 degrees, then raise it.
Begin with 5 to 6 times and
build up to 20 to 30.

Ice skating and roller skating also require firm lateral pushing
motions that are helpful in conditioning. They are also good aerobic
sports and will keep your heart in shape during the off-season. You
can also make up certain exercises such as hopping back and forth
over a low bench or your racket. To significantly increase power,
use a weight boot and practice abduction while lying on a floor
and adduction using a bench (Figures 2-8 and 2-9). The straddle

Figure 2-10   Straddle hops are just like jumping jacks except you carry a 10-pound barbell on your shoulders to increase the resistance. Here, starting with 5 and building to 10 repetitions is sufficient.

hop with a barbell or holding dumbbells (in essence, a modification of jumping jacks) is also a useful exercise (Figure 2-10). Flexibility is especially important for prevention of groin injuries and is discussed in the next chapter.

Isometric exercises for the lower leg are very convenient and helpful, especially if you are having problems with your knee (for example, chondromalacia) or with the adductor and abductor muscles of the thigh. They can be done during the day while sitting in a chair (Figure 2-11). For your knee (quadriceps muscles) do 10 repetitions of 7 seconds each with a 3-second rest, holding your knee out in successive 10-degree elevations from 80 degrees of flexion to full extension. For adductor and abductor muscles do the exercise illustrated in Figure 2-12 for 10 seconds. Exercises for the leg are summarized in Table 2-1.

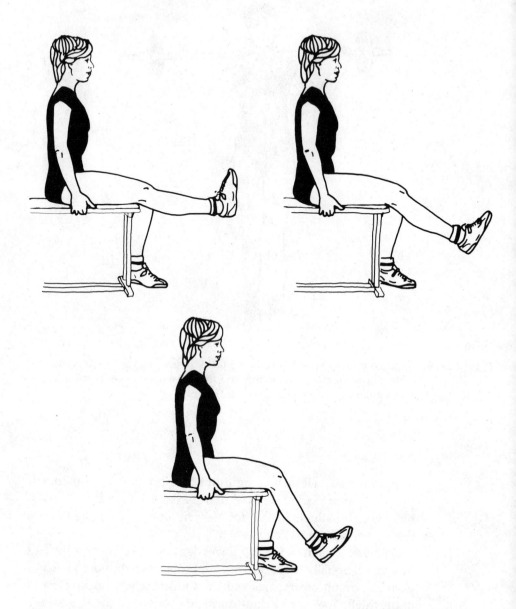

Figure 2-11 Isometric quadriceps exercises, done at successive 10-degree arcs.

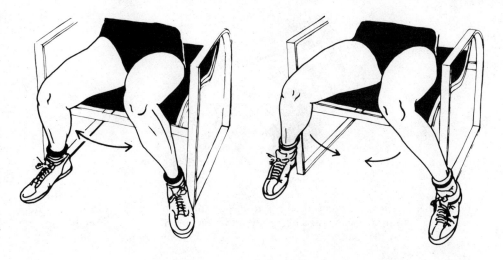

Figure 2-12 Sit with your feet pressing against the front legs of a chair. By pressing inward, your adduction muscles are isometrically strengthened. By pressing outward, your hip abductors are strengthened.

Table 2-1 Exercises for the legs

Muscle Group	Resistance	Mixed	Endurance
Calf	Sitting toe-ups with barbell (Figure 2-2)	Straddle hops (Figure 2-10) Sprinting	Jogging Jumping jacks (Figure 2-7)
Quadriceps	Squats (Figure 2-4) Leg extension (Figure 2-5)	Knee-bends	Bicycling Hill running
Hamstrings	Leg curls (Figure 2-6)		Jogging
Groin	Abduction and adduction with weight boot (Figures 2-8 and 2-9)	Straddle hops (Figure 2-10)	Jumping jacks Skating

The Lower Back and Abdomen

Getting your back into shape and keeping it that way involves much more than simple strengthening exercises, as shown by the millions of words written about it. Obviously what we say here is only an outline, designed for the person with a healthy back who wants to keep it that way.

Proper function of your lower back depends on stretching exercises (Chapter 3) as much as on strength and on proper care of the

Figure 2-13 Anchor your feet, hold a 5- to 10-pound weight behind your head, bend your knees and slowly curl up and then curl down again. Begin with 5 to 10 repetitions and build to 50 before increasing the weight.

contiguous areas of your anatomy—abdomen, pelvic girdle, and thighs—and of your back itself. Chapter 9 will pull all of this together. Here, we will discuss exercises designed to increase the strength of your back, abdomen, thighs, and buttock muscles.

The abdomen shares responsibility with the back for supporting the upper trunk. Together, if in good shape, they form a muscular cylinder to carry the upper body—but if the abdomen is weak, all the weight falls on the back and spinal column, which are not designed to carry the load by themselves. Abdominal and anterior thigh strength is best developed by sit-ups. By doing sit-ups with your knees bent, you isolate and exercise the abdominal muscles during the initial portion of the sit-up and the anterior thigh muscles at the end. When they are done with legs held straight, the first 15 to 25 degrees of the sit-up exercises the psoas musculature, which attaches to the back. You should avoid doing sit-ups this way, especially if your back is injured. The proper way to do sit-ups is with bent knees. Build up to the point where you can do at least 25 sit-ups, and then add to the mechanical disadvantage by putting your hands behind your head and even carrying a small 5- to 10-pound weight (Figure 2-13). Using a slant board further increases the difficulty of the exercise, but it is probably not necessary for most tennis players, since you can develop a firm abdomen with conventional sit-ups.

The oblique muscles of the abdomen are developed by doing rotational exercises with a broomstick (Figure 2-14) or by touching your elbows to the opposite knee during sit-ups (Figure 2-15).

Figure 2-14 Oblique muscles of your abdominal wall (along either side and flank) are developed by this exercise, one of the easiest. The only trick is to twist smoothly and as far as you can go easily.

The simplest exercise for your lower back is to touch your toes. To avoid injuries, this should be done slowly with your knees slightly bent; stay down for 10 seconds, and straighten up slowly. Never bounce up and down. The stretch helps loosen your back, and the return to upright posture strengthens the muscles of the spine and buttocks. Despite its simplicity, you must be very careful with this exercise if you have any back trouble (Chapter 9).

If your back is healthy, you can do a variation of this exercise with weights while you are sitting (Figure 2-16). Carry a barbell on your shoulders, bend forward until your upper body touches your thighs, and then straighten out. It can also be done standing, in which case it is called the ''good morning'' exercise. It should be done with knees slightly flexed to avoid back injuries.

Free weights offer the only safe means generally available to

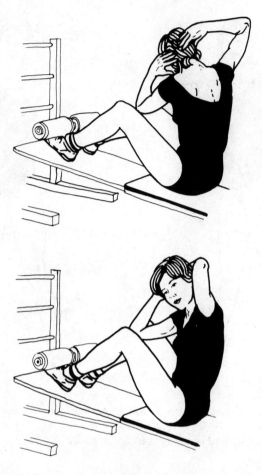

Figure 2-15 Rotational sit-ups. Start your sit-up normally, but finish it by rotating and touching elbow to opposite knee. Alternate right and left with each sit-up.

Table 2-2 Strength exercises for the back and adjacent muscles

Muscles	Resistance	Calisthenics
Abdominal (including anterior thigh)	Bent knee sit-ups with weight or on oblique board (Figure 2-13)	Bent knee sit-ups
Abdominal oblique		Rotational sit-ups (Figure 2-15) Twists (Figure 2-14)
Lower back (including buttocks)	Good morning exercises (Figure 2-16)	Toe-touches

Figure 2-16 ''Good morning'' exercise for back flexion is done with a 5- to 10-pound barbell resting across the shoulder. **A,** Sit on a bench as illustrated. Bend over until your upper body is parallel to the floor. Return to starting position. Repeat 6 to 10 times. **B,** Stand with your knees slightly flexed.

provide resistance training for your back. Many equipment manufacturers offer apparatus that allows you to perform so-called extension exercises. Although these are good, dynamic back exercises, they should be done only after you have already developed considerable strength in your back and should *never* be done if you have back pain; they should be avoided by the average tennis player. Exercises for the back and adjacent muscles are summarized in Table 2-2.

The Upper Body: Upper Back, Shoulders, Arms, and Chest

The muscles of your upper back are responsible for the movement of your shoulders and arms. In that sense they are really extensions of the upper extremities and are affected by all exercises of the arms and shoulders. The key muscles are biceps, triceps, rotator cuff, chest (or pectoral) muscles, and the muscles along the side of the back that attach to the upper arm, the latissimus dorsi or "lats." These are the muscles used in your strokes. We will mention the most important and typical exercises here.

Even though there may still be controversy about combining swimming and tennis, swimming is one of the most useful forms of conditioning and endurance exercise for your upper body. The crawl develops the chest (pectoral) and anterior shoulder (deltoid) muscles, which are used in service and forearm strokes. The breaststroke helps develop the lateral and posterior shoulder muscles and the latissimus dorsi, the major muscles of the upper back. The full range of motion used in swimming is especially valuable.

If you are a landlubber, you can do calisthenics for shoulder, chest, and arm strength. Push-ups will build your triceps, chest, and shoulders, and chin-ups will develop your back and biceps. Windmill calisthenics exercise all the muscles around the shoulder (Figure 2-17).

For most of us, exercises using dumbbells or barbells provide sufficient resistance training for tennis. The best resistance exercise for your backhand is the "bent-over lateral raise" (Figure 2-18). It exercises your lower back as well and should not be done if you have any pain (an alternate method is given later). Hold a dumbbell in each hand, bend over from the waist, and bring the dumbbells straight out to your side until they are positioned above your torso. Slowly return to starting position and repeat. If the exercise bothers your back, you can do it while sitting or lying prone on a weight bench. This exercise translates directly into increased backhand strength. Most women should start with about 5 pounds, men with 10 to 15 pounds. If it is overdone, you could get pain in the shoulder, so build up very slowly.

Figure 2-17 Windmills can be done one arm at a time or both simultaneously, forward or backward. Slowly at first, swing your arm through a complete circle; as you get looser, speed up. Do 10 to 25 on each side.

The opposite exercise, "lying, straight-arm lateral raises," or flies, is done while lying on your back on a bench. Hold the same dumbbells above you at arm's length. Keeping your arms locked, slowly lower them to the side, allowing them to drop as low as is comfortable (Figure 2-19). Then return to the starting position. The same exercise can be done with your arms bent, reducing the mechanical disadvantage and decreasing the strain.

An excellent exercise for the triceps is the French press because it simulates the position of the upper arm during service. Hold a dumbbell in one hand directly over your head. Slowly bring the dumbbell down in a semicircle to the back of your neck, moving only your forearm and keeping your upper arm and elbow stationary. Return to the starting position. You should do it with each arm to maintain muscular balance, or you can do it with a barbell using

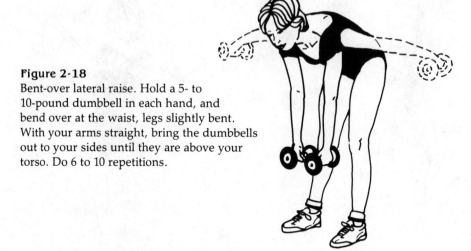

Figure 2-18
Bent-over lateral raise. Hold a 5- to
10-pound dumbbell in each hand, and
bend over at the waist, legs slightly bent.
With your arms straight, bring the dumbbells
out to your sides until they are above your
torso. Do 6 to 10 repetitions.

Figure 2-19
Lying, straight-arm lateral raise.
Lying on your back, hold 5- to
10-pound dumbbells above your
chest at arm's length. Keep your
arms straight, and slowly lower
the dumbbells to your sides.
Return to the starting
position and repeat 6 to
10 times.

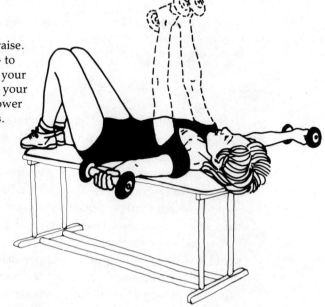

Figure 2-20 French press. This is the basic exercise for the triceps. Stand and hold a barbell or dumbbells over your head with your arms straight. Keep your upper arms and elbows stationary, and lower the barbell to the back of your neck, moving only your forearms. Slowly return to starting position. Repeat 6 to 10 times. Do on both sides.

both arms at once (Figure 2-20). All "press" exercises, including bench, military, and behind the neck, strengthen the triceps as well.

The biceps are developed by so-called curls, which can be done in many ways. We prefer using dumbbells because they require greater action of the wrist and hand. If you do this exercise standing with your back against a wall, you can concentrate all the effort on the biceps. Using two dumbbells together, hold them at your side, and then slowly and deliberately curl them up to your upper chest. You can also use a barbell, as shown in Figure 2-21. A variation with your hands over the top of the weight is called a reverse curl and is also very useful to develop the brachialis muscle, since the biceps are less effective with the forearm in this position.

A separate exercise should be done for the anterior part of the

Figure 2-21 Curls and reverse curls can be done with dumbbells or a barbell. **A** and **B,**
Curls are done by holding the barbell at shoulder width, palms forward,
and slowly bringing it up in a curling motion until it touches your upper
chest and neck. They exercise the biceps. **C** and **D,** Reverse curls are
done in the same manner except the bar is gripped with palms facing
backward. Reverse curls exercise the brachialis muscles of the forearm.
They should be done with the elbows held tightly to your sides. Each
exercise should be done smoothly, raising and lowering the bar slowly.
Repeat 6 to 10 times.

Figure 2-22   Front lateral raises exercise the front portion of the deltoid muscles. Use barbells or dumbbells, 2- to 5-pounds, for each arm initially. Slowly raise the barbell to shoulder height, keeping your arms straight, and smoothly return to starting position. Repeat 6 to 10 times.

shoulder. The simplest is the front lateral raise done with barbell or dumbbell. The key to this exercise is to keep your arms stiff through the full range of motion. Stand with the weight across the upper thighs and slowly raise the barbell in a circular path until it is at shoulder height; return to starting position (Figure 2-22).

The forearm. Weight training for the forearm is very easily done and yet is probably the most important exercise in tennis. The basic exercise is the wrist curl, both with palms up and with palms down (reverse wrist curl). The key to this exercise is good support for your forearm during the exercise. It is convenient to do it while sitting, using either a barbell or two dumbbells. On the standard curl, hold the barbell about shoulder's width with hands facing up. Slowly allow your wrists to drop down as far as they will go; then curl the bar back up as high as possible; finally, return to the starting position

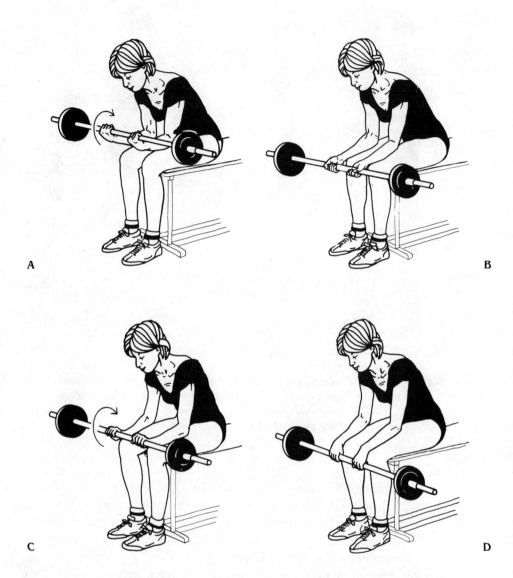

Figure 2-23 Sit comfortably on a bench, rest your forearms on your thighs with palms face up for curls (**A** and **B**) and face down for reverse curls (**C** and **D**). For curls, slowly bend your wrists and hands down as far as they will go, and then curl the bar up as far as possible, holding your arms still and using only your wrists. For reverse curls, do the same thing palms down. Do 15 to 30 repetitions using as little as 2 to 5 pounds of weight initially.

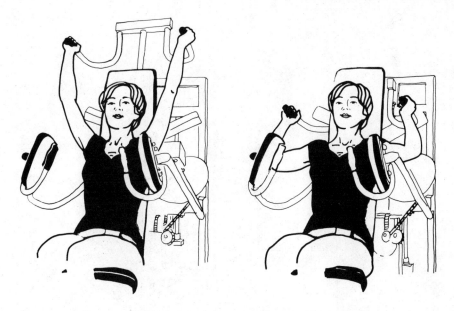

Figure 2-24 Nautilus press exercises your triceps. Grip the bench press station handles, and slowly straighten your arms so that you are supporting the handles at arm's length over your head. Then slowly lower them again. Pick a weight that allows you to do six repetitions initially.

(Figure 2-23). A set of these exercises is about 20 repetitions. Begin by using a 10- to 20-pound barbell or 5- to 10-pound dumbbell for men, and half that weight for women.

For reverse wrist curls, do the same motion but hold the weight with your palms down. This exercise is especially important for the prevention of tennis elbow, but it should not be done if you have an acute tennis elbow. You'll find, however, that you can manage about half as much weight with your palms down as with them up.

For variety and flexibility, wrist rotations done with dumbbells while your arms are in the curl position will help increase wrist strength and quickness, especially if you have begun to add spin to your shots.

Finally, don't neglect your hands. A set of spring-loaded hand or grip strengtheners will add to forearm, hand, and finger strength. Build up until you can do 100 repetitions.

Exercise machines for the upper body. Upper body exercises for tennis are so simple that all you need are barbells and a bench.

Figure 2-25   Nautilus pull-down. The range of motion is very great, with your arms going through 200 degrees. The technique should be taught by a coach, since improper use of this machine can injure the shoulder.

However, some exercise equipment can be useful if you want to try it, especially for some supplemental exercises designed to maximize strength.

The bench press—working the pectoral, deltoid, and triceps muscles—is considered a basic upper body exercise. It is considerably easier to do with a Universal Gym or Nautilus machine (Figure 2-24) than with free weights. Pull-downs develop the latissimus muscles. The Nautilus pull-down machine emphasizes a very full range of motion (Figure 2-25).

Nautilus has other machines that are useful for tennis players. One in particular allows you to do the equivalent of lying lateral raises with minimum strain on the back and is useful when working with high resistance (Figure 2-26). Exercises for the upper body are summarized in Table 2-3.

Table 2-3   Exercises for the upper body

Muscle Group	Resistance	Mixed	Endurance
Shoulder, upper back, and chest	Bent-over lateral raises (Figure 2-18) Lying lateral raises (Figure 2-19) Chest machine (Figure 2-26) Front lateral raises (Figure 2-22) Press machine (Figure 2-24)	Push-ups	Swimming Windmills (Figure 2-17)
Latissimus dorsi	Pull-down machine (Figure 2-25)	Chin-ups	Swimming (breaststroke and backstroke)
Triceps	French press (Figure 2-20) Press machine (Figure 2-24)	Push-ups	
Biceps	Arm curls (Figure 2-21)	Chin-ups	
Forearm	Reverse arm curls Wrist curls (Figure 2-23) Reverse wrist curls Wrist rotations	Reverse chin-ups	
Hands	Grip strengtheners		

Exercise Programs

We've illustrated a great number of exercises. Clearly, you can't—and shouldn't—do them all; nor should you perform selected exercises in a random manner. What you need is a careful program. Conditioning programs for tennis should emphasize the following: aerobic (or endurance) exercise for your legs and cardiovascular system and calisthenics and resistance exercise for your knees, groin, back, abdomen, shoulder, and forearms. We will demonstrate programs for several ability levels, but first we must emphasize an important provision: whether you use exercise machines or free weights, it is crucial to have good hands-on instruction by a knowledgeable coach for proper technique and for safety.

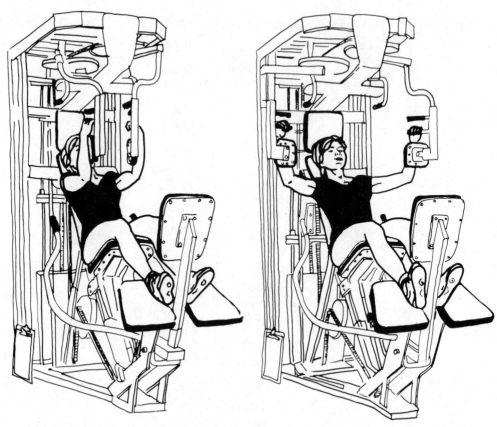

Figure 2-26 Nautilus chest exercise is similar to lying lateral raises. Pick a weight that allows six repetitions.

To help you decide which exercises to do and when to do them, we suggest that you assign yourself to one of two groups: (1) the club player who wants to devote most of his time to improving his game and strokes but wants to develop the strength and endurance to avoid injury and third-set blues or (2) the competitive player with full confidence in his game and strokes who now is working for the endurance, strength, and stamina that will provide a winning margin. Both groups should still put major emphasis on hitting shots—forehands, backhand, volley, service (the more the better, if you build up slowly; that is, don't go out for the first time in 6 months and hit 300 serves). Remember, muscle strength and endurance are *specific*, so exercising the muscles you are going to use in tennis is essential.

Group One: General Conditioning for Club-level Players

A. **Off-season conditioning:** If you are playing 0 to 4 times per month, use the following program to stay in shape.

Aerobics: Modify according to weather, region, facilities, and personal preference.

Jogging—no sprints	2 to 3 miles, 3 to 5 times per week; 6 to 15 miles per week

Optional substitutes

Exercise bicycle	30 minutes
Bicycling	3 to 6 miles
Ice skating	30 minutes
Swimming	½ mile
Cross-country skiing	2 to 5 miles
Jumping rope	10 to 20 minutes

Calisthenics: Do 3 to 6 times per week.

Partial knee-bends	10 to 20
Toe-touches	10
Sit-ups, including some twists	25 to 50
Push-ups	20 to 30
Jumping jacks	50 to 100

Resistance: Lift 1 or 2 times per week, after your aerobics; do not lift on days when you play or do calisthenics.

Wrist curls, regular and reversed
Arm curls
French press
Lying lateral raises

B. **Preseason conditioning:** Begin 1 or 2 months before the season begins. The major emphasis should be to increase your speed and stroking power. Add the following to above regimen.

Sprinting	10 to 50 yards, at 90% maximum; build to 1000 yards total, 1 or 2 times per week
Practice serves	Start with 25, build to 100
Good morning exercises	6 to 10 repetitions, 1 set
Lying lateral raises	6 to 10 repetitions, 1 to 3 sets

C. **Season:** If you are playing 3 to 6 times per week, use the following program.

Aerobics: Cut down jogging to 5 to 10 miles per week—about 2 miles per day when not playing; discontinue sprints.

Calisthenics: Continue, use as warm-up for games.

Resistance: Continue only on days when not playing, and do not increase weight or repetitions.

Group Two: Advanced Conditioning for Full-time Players

There is no real season; rather, the emphasis should be to get into shape and maintain it year round. An hour per day put into conditioning in addition to your tennis is reasonable. On weeks that you play competitively, cut your running to about half your distance and eliminate sprints. Do not lift weights at least 48 hours before a match.

Aerobics: There is no substitute for running, but you can supplement it with other aerobics, especially swimming, bicycling, and jumping rope.

Jogging	5 to 6 miles, 4 to 6 times per week; 20 to 25 miles per week
Sprinting	10 to 50 yards at 90% maximum; build to 1000 yards, 1 to 2 times per week

Calisthenics

Partial knee-bends	20 to 40
Toe-touches	10 to 20
Sit-ups	25 to 50
Push-ups	30 to 40
Jumping jacks	100 to 200
Chin-ups	20 to 30

Resistance: Do 6 to 10 repetitions, 3 sets.
Sitting toe-ups
Squats
Good morning exercises
Lying lateral raises
French press
Bench press
Arm curls, regular and reversed
Wrist curls, regular and reversed
Pull-down exercises

3 Improving Your Range: A Program to Increase Flexibility for Tennis

Stretching

Stretching is as natural as yawning. For centuries stretching has been an integral part of ballet training, but only in recent years has it been recognized as an important type of exercise for athletes. Unfortunately, tennis players have lagged far behind other athletes in discovering the benefits of stretching. Today any progressive exercise regimen should include a careful program of stretching before and after your other exercises.

Stretching increases flexibility, and flexibility is necessary for you to maintain a full range of motion, to be able to reach the ball and hit it smoothly. Flexibility also protects you from injuries. Different people have different degrees of flexibility, but the more you play tennis and the stronger your muscles become, the tighter they are—and the more important it is that you do a regular set of stretching exercises.

Stretching exercises can be *dynamic* or *static*. Dynamic stretching is done by moving a limb to the point of tightness and then relaxing. Static stretching is done by moving to the point of tightness and holding that position for 5 to 30 seconds. Most dynamic stretches come from calisthenics (for example, toe-touching develops good hamstring and lower back flexibility), whereas many static stretches are derived from dance or from various Yoga positions. By and large, static stretching exercises have gained favor in recent years, but the evidence is not convincing that one way or the other is better. Our emphasis will be on static stretching exercises, but the calisthenics outlined in the previous chapter provide some dynamic stretches that complement the program recommended here.

Before discussing specifics, we should mention a few general rules. Stretching should be done slowly, to the point of tightness. If it hurts, you've gone too far. Correcting inflexibility takes time. Don't try to change years of inactivity in a few weeks, and don't bounce: tight muscles can be torn by hard, sudden pulls. Slow, steady, and easy are the basic principles of all stretching.

Conditioning for tennis requires attention to your entire body, so we will proceed anatomically from area to area. For most regions we will provide a self-test to tell you how tight you are and a set of stretches to correct the inflexibility.

The Lower Leg

In the lower leg the main areas that need stretching are the muscles of the calf and the Achilles tendon. The stretch and the test are identical. Begin with your calf (Figure 3-1, *A*). Stretch your calf by standing 2 to 3 feet away from a wall. Move one foot forward. Lean forward against the wall, bending the back leg at the ankle and keeping your knee straight. Keep your toes straight ahead and heels flat. You should be able to make a 45-degree angle between your back leg and the ground. Hold the stretch for approximately 30 seconds, then repeat on your other leg.

Next, step forward with one foot, and bend both your knees slightly while you lean against the wall (Figure 3-1, *B*). That should allow you another 5 to 10 degrees of motion and transfer the stretch to the Achilles tendon and soleus muscle. Lean forward gently, and hold at the point you feel tight for 10 to 20 seconds.

A calf stretch can also be done on a stair (Figure 3-1, *C*). Put the ball of your foot on the edge of a stair, and slowly allow your heel to drop below the stair level while holding onto the railing for balance. Do not bounce or suddenly put your full weight on the back of your feet. Here you can see the virtue of slow, static stretches, since this one, done too rapidly with your full weight coming down, can lead to a muscle pull.

Some stretching exercises can be done almost anywhere without attracting undue attention; calf and Achilles tendon stretches are among these. For example, you can lean against a wall while waiting for an elevator (if you still use elevators instead of stairs).

If you are suffering from shin splints, in addition to paying particular attention to stretching your Achilles tendon and calf, a stretching exercise for your anterior shin muscles, the warrior's

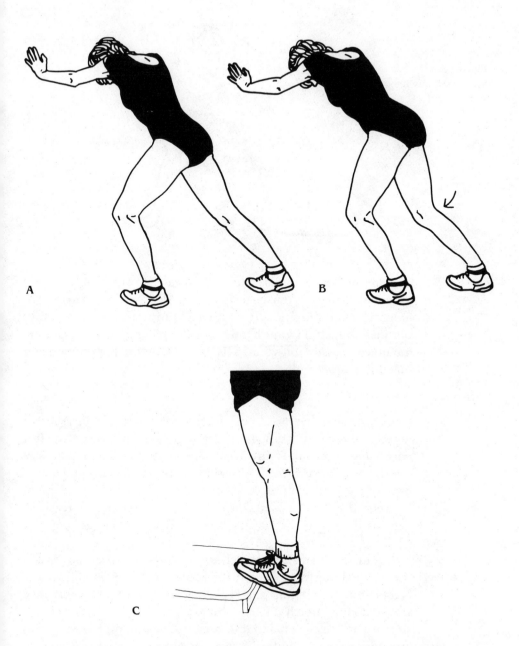

Figure 3-1 Calf and Achilles tendon. **A,** Calf stretch and self-test. **B,** Achilles tendon stretch. **C,** Stair stretch.

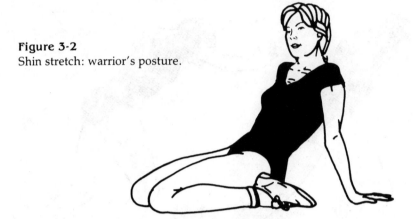

Figure 3-2
Shin stretch: warrior's posture.

posture, may be helpful (Figure 3-2). It can be surprisingly hard to do initially. Sit on your heel. If your ankles are tight, move your foot slightly to the side and your weight forward somewhat, supporting yourself on your hands if necessary and avoiding putting too much pressure on your heels. Find a comfortable position and hold it for 20 seconds.

The Thigh

Hamstring stretches are difficult for most of us because these strong muscles at the back of the thigh are large and hard to stretch. Test yourself as shown in Figure 3-3, *A*. Lie on your back with your legs out straight. Have a friend raise one leg until you feel a pull on the back of the leg or until your knee bends. Estimate the degrees between the floor and your leg. You should be able to reach 90 degrees, but don't be surprised if you have trouble getting past 45 degrees.

The simplest hamstring stretch is a gentle toe-touch (if your back is sound), holding the position for approximately 5 to 10 seconds before straightening up and repeating the stretch. An alternative way to do this stretch is while sitting (Figure 3-3, *B*), which is much safer if you have even a hint of back trouble. Sit on the floor with legs outstretched, and lean forward to grab your ankles. If you are like most of us, at the start you won't be able to do that without bending your knees. Loop a towel around your feet and use it to pull yourself as far forward as possible, keeping your knees straight. Stretch for 30 seconds, then relax. As you become more flexible,

Figure 3-3   Hamstrings. **A,** Self-test. **B,** Sitting hamstring stretch. **C,** One-legged hamstring stretch.

Figure 3-4   Quadriceps. **A,** Self-test and full knee flexion stretch. **B,** Extension of quadriceps stretch to reach anterior thigh muscles.

you will be able to dispense with the towel. Finally, if you have very tight hamstrings, you can stretch them by putting one leg at a time on a bar or chair and leaning forward (Figure 3-3, *C*). Hold for 30 seconds and switch sides.

The quadriceps muscles at the front of your thigh are also prone to inflexibility. You should be able to pull your foot up behind and kick yourself in the buttocks (Figure 3-4, *A*). If you can't, your quadriceps are too tight; you need to do this test as a stretch, holding it for at least 20 seconds before releasing. A variation of this stretch is done while lying prone. Bend one leg back, and hold your foot while you lean back. Use your arms for support. The further back you lean, the more stretch you place on your anterior thigh muscles

Figure 3-5 Hurdler's stretch.

(Figure 3-4, *B*). After you've achieved a certain amount of flexibility in your upper leg, you can try the hurdler's stretch (Figure 3-5). This is a good stretch combining quadriceps, ankle, and hamstring stretch for those with moderately good flexibility. Sit with one leg bent back and your knee to the side. Reach forward and touch the toes of the outstretched leg. As you get better, bring your body closer to the straight leg while placing the bent knee at a greater angle. Do this stretch for both legs.

The Groin

As a first exercise for the groin and also a self-test sit on the floor with your feet together. Lean forward and apply gentle pressure to your knees, pushing them toward the floor (Figure 3-6, *A*). You should be able to get your knees very close to the floor. Hold for 30 seconds. Another exercise involves some of the lower abdomen and anterior thigh muscles as well (Figure 3-6, *B*). The key to this stretch is to have your knee above your ankle to start, and then lower your hips gradually to create tension and stretch the muscles of the groin. Use your hands for balance. Hold for 15 seconds, and reverse sides. It is difficult to achieve a gentle stretch here without bouncing, but this is an important stretch, so work at it. Figure 3-6, *C*, shows a stretch that is hard to do but very beneficial for the groin. Begin this stretch by learning to sit comfortably on the floor with your back straight and your legs straight and spread apart. When you are able to hold this position, you can begin to bend directly forward from the hips and to bend toward either leg. You should feel this stretch in the groin and hamstrings. Hold for 30 to 40 seconds.

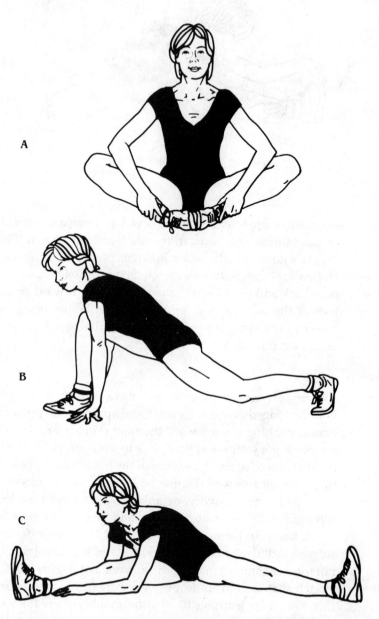

Figure 3-6   Groin. **A,** Sitting stretch and self-test. **B,** Starting position stretch. **C,** Sitting spread-leg stretch.

The Lower Back

The lower back is effectively loosened by two basic types of stretches. One is the toe-touch, which affects the pelvic girdle primarily but also helps the hamstrings and the muscles along the spine (Figure 3-7, *A*). The toe-touch is also the best test for your back and pelvic flexibility. The more flexible you are, the further down you can reach. To do the exercise, slowly bend forward from the hips. The key is to allow your back to gently round and to slightly bend your knees to avoid stressing your lower back. Stretch until you begin to feel tightness in the back of your legs, and hold for 20 seconds. Do not bounce, and do not force it. Over a period of days you will gradually loosen up and eventually be able to touch the floor. There is also a correct way to straighten up. As illustrated, round your back again and bend your knees somewhat more. This allows a smooth pelvic rotation without undue back strain and makes this a safe stretch.

Another back exercise is a form of *pelvic tilt* designed principally to pull on the muscles along the spine (Figure 3-7, *B*), gently stretching them while reversing the normal curvature of the lower back. While lying on your back, bring one leg up at a time, pulling it gently to your chest, or do both legs at once. You can do this exercise in bed before getting up the day after a hard game.

A third exercise, called the *cat's back*, should be reserved for those without back pain. It will gradually greatly increase the flexibility in your lower back. Position yourself on your hands and knees (Figure 3-7, *C*). Gently round your back as much as you can. Think of a cat arching its back. Then slowly reverse and try to lower your back as much as possible to an almost swaybacked position. Repeat four or five times. Rotational exercises, similar to those illustrated in Chapter 2, will enhance the degree to which your trunk can twist in preparing to hit a ball. Using a broom handle or outstretched arms, gently rotate as far as possible to one side (Figure 3-7, *D*), then the other. Repeat 5 to 10 times. Combined with partial knee-bends at the end of a rotation (Figure 3-7, *E*), this is a very effective warm-up exercise. You should feel like you're winding yourself up, uncurling as you straighten, and winding up again on the other side.

The Shoulder and Upper Back

To test your shoulder and upper back, grasp one hand with the other behind your back as shown in Figure 3-8, *A* and *B*. When you

Figure 3-7 Lower back. **A,** Proper toe-touch maneuvers and self-test. **B,** William's pelvic tilts with single knee and both knees. **C,** Cat's back.

D, Trunk rotation. **E,** Twisting knee-bends.

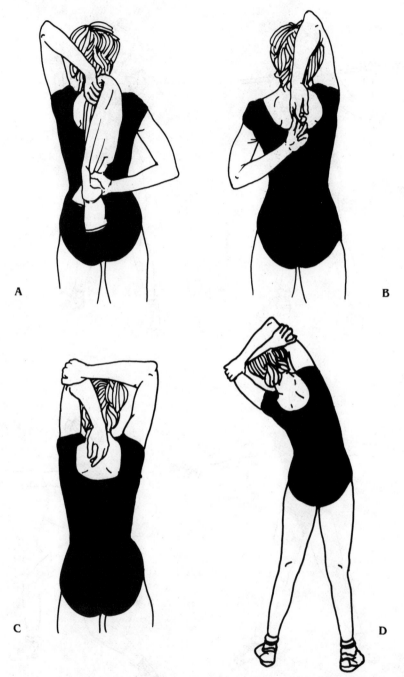

Figure 3-8   Shoulder and upper back. **A** and **B,** Self-test and shoulder stretch with hands behind back, with and without towel. **C,** Shoulder stretch, one-sided. **D,** Leaning shoulder, lateral back stretch.

are flexible, you should be able to reach behind your head with either hand and grab the other one coming up. Most of us will have problems bringing the dominant hand (right side for right-handed people) up enough because of the tightness in the shoulders. If so, use a towel, dropping it from the upper hand and grabbing it with the lower hand. This allows you to bring gentle tension to bear on your shoulders, gradually stretching the muscles. Hold for 20 seconds, and reverse positions. Don't force this stretch. A supplementary exercise where you *gently* apply pressure to the elbow of your upraised arm to help stretch it out is shown in Figure 3-8, *C*. You can do a similar maneuver with your arm down and behind the back, reaching across to gently pull it further. A variation of this exercise (Figure 3-8, *D*), where you also lean to the side, stretches the large muscle of the upper back, the latissimus dorsi. Grab your elbows behind your head, and bend from your hips to the side. Bend your knees slightly. Hold for 30 seconds. Repeat for the other side.

You can stretch the front of your shoulder and chest by linking your hands behind your back with your elbows inward and raising

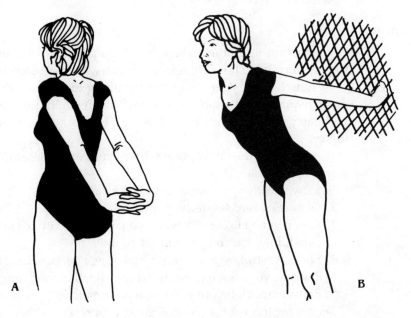

Figure 3-9   Anterior shoulder and chest. **A,** Linked hands, behind back. **B,** Fence grab.

them as high as possible (Figure 3-9, *A*). Do it also with your hands separated, especially if you have a linked fence to grab, so that you gently allow your weight to fall forward (Figure 3-9, *B*).

When to Stretch

Now you know *how* and *why* you should stretch, but *when* should you do it? On both your playing and nonplaying days, stretching first thing in the morning is an efficient way to get started. It can be especially helpful if you played a hard match the day before and are very sore and creaky getting out of bed. As you develop your favorite stretching routine, you may also find that stretching at night before bed or while watching the late news is a relaxing way to get ready for bed. If you are doing weight training, stretching before and afterward is excellent for warming up and cooling down. You should stretch daily, if at all possible, and try different patterns and times to find the best one for you.

On playing days, stretching should become one of the cornerstones of your warm-up and cool-down regimens. Most tennis players are sadly deficient in their warm-ups, just hitting a few practice shots before starting the game. We strongly suggest that you arrive early and warm up properly, and take a few minutes at the end to cool down and stretch again.

Warm-up

A good warm-up routine will prepare you physically and mentally to play your best. It will loosen your joints, increase blood flow to your muscles, get your pulse and breathing to the pace that your game requires, and establish your rhythm. Ten minutes spent here will pay great dividends in improving your game and preventing injury.

To achieve all this, incorporate these types of exercises into your warm-up program:
   1. Slow, steady stretches to loosen your muscles
   2. Dynamic exercises derived from calisthenics
   3. Easy running to literally warm your muscles with the increased blood flow that comes from active motion
   4. Shadow strokes and then a full range of practice shots to improve your timing, eye-hand coordination, and range
   5. Repeat stretch before you begin your match

Do not neglect your serve. Powering your serves without enough practice shots to warm up will be more damaging to you than to your opponent. On cool days be sure to wear warm clothing to start; as you warm up, you can shed layers until you are dressed for playing.

The order in which to do this warm-up routine is up to you, although we prefer stretching, calisthenics, jogging, hitting, and finishing off by stretching again, as follows:

Stretches (2 minutes)
    Calf and Achilles tendon stretches
    Hamstring stretch
    Groin stretch
    Shoulder stretch

Calisthenics (2 minutes)
    Partial knee-bends
    Jumping jacks
    Toe-touches, alternate toes, with reach back
    Twisting knee-bends
    Windmills, forward and backward

Jog 1 to 2 minutes to point of sweating (baseline to net at gradually increased speed)

Hitting (including many serves and overhand strokes)

Repeat stretches (before you begin your match; 2 minutes)
    Calf and Achilles tendon stretches
    Twists
    Toe-touches with reach back
    Windmills

Cool-down

After you play, a cool-down period will help keep your muscles from tightening up, protect your circulation, and clear the waste products of energy metabolism from your muscles. First, put on your sweat suit, then go through a gentle calisthenic routine, and finally, repeat your stretching exercises. If you have been playing hard enough to be out of breath, walk for a few minutes first until your heart and breathing rate come down. Incorporating a warm-up and cool-down period into your game takes only a few extra minutes, and it is truly the ounce of prevention.

Summary

There you have it: a set of 10 to 12 fundamental exercises, taking 5 to 10 minutes, which will allow you to achieve and maintain a full range of motion for all your joints and substantially reduce the chances of injury. A few minutes of stretching may save you weeks of discomfort. In addition, your reach will be extended and your strokes and follow-through will be smoother and more fluid. Finally, stretching will decrease the tension and tightness in your muscles so you'll feel more relaxed on and off the court.

Common Tennis Problems: Recognition, Treatment, and Rehabilitation

4   Head and Neck Injuries

Every experienced player is well aware of the importance of strategy in winning tennis. In this context the dictum "use your head" is a familiar exhortation of coaches and teaching pros everywhere. Similarly, one of the first principles of good tennis technique is to keep your eye on the ball. This, too, is good advice. From a medical point of view, however, it is more important to know how to keep the ball out of your eye and how to protect your head and neck while playing tennis. Head and neck problems are actually less common than other tennis-related injuries. However, they can be quite serious when they do occur. Although many tennis problems cannot be completely eliminated even with the utmost care, eye injuries can be prevented by using protective equipment.

Headaches

Headaches can be caused by many different factors. Perhaps the most common causes of headaches during a game are *heat and dehydration*. Needless to say, this is most likely to occur during intense play in warm summer weather. Direct sun exposure can contribute to this type of headache, but you are better off using a visor for protection instead of a hat; a visor will shade your eyes and face from the sun while still allowing heat to escape from the rest of your head. The answer to dehydration is also quite obvious: fluid replacement. Details about protection from sun and heat are given in Chapter 12 and about fluid replacement in Chapters 12 and 15.

Avoiding the midday sun and ensuring adequate fluid replacement will prevent most lightheadedness, dizziness, and headaches on the tennis court. If your headaches persist despite these precautions, you should investigate other possible causes. *Tension* is one common cause of headaches. Tennis is a competitive game, and hard-fought contests are part of the fun. Even so, it is possible to take your tennis too seriously. If you find that your concentration is so intense that you get tension headaches, you should rethink your tennis philosophy. You should work hard in practice, play hard in competition, and relax thoroughly when the match is over. Don't fight your way up your club's tennis ladder if each rung causes nervousness and headaches.

Eye strain is another cause of headaches in tennis players. Visual concentration is extremely important for the successful player. Visual acuity, depth perception, and the ability to focus and shift focus rapidly are necessary to pick up the ball early, detect its trajectory, and even estimate its spin and bounce. All this can cause eye strain, which may produce headaches. Your ophthalmologist may be able to help by prescribing corrective lenses. If you suffer from headaches or eye strain (or if you just feel that you are seeing the ball late), have a checkup to be sure that your problem isn't poor vision, poor depth perception, or eye muscle strain.

Finally, *glare* can cause headaches. Although bright sunlight is the chief offender, don't be lulled into a false sense of security by high clouds, since glare can be substantial even on hazy days. A sun visor may help, but if you are still troubled by glare, you should try sunglasses. Use only safety lenses so that your eyes are protected from impact injuries. Gray or brown lenses distort colors less and are therefore preferable; green lenses are also acceptable, but faddish sunglasses of yellow, blue, or pink distort color perception and should be avoided. Polarizing lenses reduce glare and are also desirable. Phototrophic lenses, which automatically adjust to glare by becoming darker in brighter light, are ideal but are more expensive than ordinary sunglasses.

Once you have a headache, you will be more interested in treatment than prevention. Most headaches will respond to aspirin or acetaminophen (Tylenol and other brands). If your headache is mild, you can take the tablets and continue to play. But if you are in moderate or severe discomfort, you should stop playing and rest in cool, dark, quiet surroundings until you are better.

The majority of headaches are not medically serious. However, if you are subject to severe or recurrent headaches, you should see your doctor. This is particularly true if the headaches are accompanied by other neurologic symptoms such as forgetfulness, personality changes, visual disturbances, dizziness, loss of coordination, weakness, or numbness. Your doctor will try to determine the reasons for your headaches so that the proper treatment can be initiated. Many new approaches are available, particularly for migraine headaches, which can be disabling without treatment.

Eye Injuries

Eye injuries pose potentially important problems for the tennis player. The National Society to Prevent Blindness estimates that at least 25,000 sports-related eye injuries are severe enough to require treatment in hospital emergency wards in the United States each year. Of these, about 20% are caused by racquet sports, including tennis, squash, and badminton. A majority of these injuries occur in young players. These 5000 eye injuries from racquet sports vary in severity. Many are mild, but some are quite serious.

Your eye is surrounded by a group of strong bones called the *orbit*. The orbit provides protection for your eye, but unfortunately this protection is incomplete. If the bones of the orbit itself are struck by a fast-moving racquet during doubles play, a *blow-out* fracture can result. This causes pain and swelling around your eye and may damage one of the muscles that moves the eye. The result is double vision—and a trip to the operating room. If your eye itself is hit by a racquet or ball, the damage may be even greater. Deep cuts or lacerations may occur, and these too require surgery. Even if there is no laceration, bleeding into the eye (a *hyphema*) can impair vision and elevate pressure in the eye to produce glaucoma. Although this condition also can be treated surgically, vision can be permanently impaired. Another type of eye injury is a corneal abrasion or scratch. Although this usually heals well with simple patching, infections can complicate healing and corneal scars may result. Finally, trauma can cause a retinal detachment, which can lead to serious visual impairment or blindness.

The diagnosis and treatment of these eye injuries are quite technical, so you should see an ophthalmologist promptly if you sustain an eye injury on the tennis court. By far the most important thing for you to know about these injuries is that the majority of them are preventable.

Among the racquet sports, tennis is the lease dangerous because the ball is larger and softer and because the larger court size gives you time to react and to protect your eyes. But even in tennis, eye injuries can occur, especially during net play and in doubles.

If you need corrective lenses or sunglasses, you should be sure to wear only industrial-quality safety glasses; lenses made of polycarbonate plastic generally provide the best protection. These can be ordered as sunglasses or with your particular corrective prescription. In addition, they can be purchased as clear lenses so that you can get eye protection even if you don't need glasses for your vision.

At long last manufacturers of sporting equipment have recognized the importance of eye protection. As a result, a wide variety of protective devices are now available. These include older style wire or plastic cage devices without lenses and newer goggles or glasses with strong, impact-resistant polycarbonate plastic or CR39 plastic. The newer goggle styles are more expensive but provide better eye protection.

If you wear corrective eyeglasses or sunglasses when you play, high-quality safety lenses and impact-resistant frames are mandatory for tennis. If you would not otherwise wear glasses, goggles are recommended but optional for tennis; however, they are mandatory for squash and racquetball. It may take you a while to get used to the feel and appearance of goggles, but you will gain important protection, and the added security may actually enable you to play the net more aggressively.

Even the best eye protectors are no substitute for courtesy and common sense on the court. Never put a ball into play until your opponent expects it. Similarly, don't fire off an extra shot in frustration after a lost point—it is the unexpected ball that does the greatest damage. For the same reason, don't have more than one ball in play during warm-ups. Coordinate signals and strategy with your doubles partner; to prevent injuries from his racquet, you should know who is going for the ball and who is getting out of the way.

Mouth Injuries

These same simple guidelines for doubles play and court manners will go a long way toward preventing mouth injuries during tennis. Still, even the best doubles partner may occasionally catch you with a backswing, and aggressive net play is likely to earn you at least an occasional "fuzz sandwich." So you should know what to do if a stray racquet or ball hits you in the mouth.

Because your lips are very vascular, even an small cut can cause relatively brisk bleeding. Unless there is a major laceration, ice and gentle pressure should stop the bleeding within a few minutes. Even after the bleeding stops, apply ice several times during the first few hours to prevent swelling. If bleeding persists despite first aid, or if the cut seems very deep, see your dentist or a surgeon to find out if sutures are needed.

A hard blow to the mouth may actually loosen a tooth. Although this may be painful at first, it is usually more frightening than serious. If your tooth is loose, you should be sure to eat only soft solid foods and liquids for several days until the tooth tightens up again. In most cases your tooth will be fine, but if the nerve is damaged, you could need root canal work at some time in the future. Your dentist can determine this by examining you and taking dental x-ray films, which are recommended for all significant tooth injuries.

You will need help from your dentist for more serious tooth damage. Small fractures of the enamel can be treated nicely by simply polishing them out, but if one fourth to one third of the enamel is lost, your tooth will have to be restored. This sounds formidable, but the results are cosmetically excellent—and virtually no drilling is required. Unfortunately, if more than half the enamel is fractured, or if the damage runs through the nerve canal, you will need root canal treatments, a crown, or both.

The most severe dental injuries are ones in which a tooth is partially or completely knocked out of its socket. If your tooth is only partially knocked out, try to gently push it back to its natural position. If your tooth has been completely knocked out, you will have another job first—finding the tooth. Then rinse it off and carefully put it back in its socket. After either injury you should head for your dentist at once. It may be possible to save your tooth by having the dentist attach it to adjacent teeth to immobilize it while healing occurs and then perform root canal treatments.

In the past few years there has been an increasing interest in sports dentistry, or oral orthopedics. This discipline has been extremely helpful for contact sports, since custom-designed mouth guards are critically important tooth-savers. As tennis players, we do not need these devices, but you may have heard claims that mouth guards will relax your body and improve athletic performance. Unfortunately, at present there is no scientific evidence to support these claims. If you have a malocclusion or jaw pain or headaches caused by grinding your teeth (temporomandibular joint syndrome), a mouth guard may help. But if you are free of these problems, don't expect your dentist to replace your teaching pro in improving your play.

Neck Injuries

Although an erratic ground stroke or an errant smash may give even the calmest player "a pain in the neck," real neck pain is relatively uncommon in tennis players. That's the good news. The bad news is that, when neck pain occurs, it can be both severe and prolonged.

The Normal Neck

The neck is an extremely complex set of structures packed into a small space. The cervical (upper) spine is composed of the bony vertebrae and the soft, elastic discs between the vertebral bodies. The spine itself is surrounded by muscles and ligaments. Together these structures provide both stability and mobility; these muscles and ligaments are strong enough to maintain your head in the erect posture for hours, yet they are flexible and elastic enough to allow your head to move smoothly in any direction. As with all tissues, the neck muscles and joints are supplied by nerves and blood vessels, either of which can be intimately involved in producing the severe pain that can accompany neck injuries. In addition, the major nerves and vessels to the shoulders and arms pass through the neck, so neck injuries can sometimes produce pain or weakness in the arms.

Muscle Spasms

In most tennis players the neck functions so smoothly and efficiently as to escape notice altogether. But neck problems can occur either in the course of tennis or during other daily activities. The most common cause of neck pain in tennis players is muscle spasm. Spasms can occur in many ways. Typically a sudden, unexpected motion produces a severe stretching. Muscles respond to stretching by contractions, and when these contractions are unduly strong and sustained, a spasm occurs. In addition, direct muscle trauma can lead to spasm, but this is uncommon in tennis players except in the strange situation when your partner's racquet hits your neck during doubles play. Finally, pressure on a nerve can cause muscle pain, which in turn may lead to spasm.

Whatever the cause of a spasm, once it occurs, it tends to perpetuate itself. This is because the vigorous muscle contraction tends to compress blood vessels, impairing blood flow to the muscle just at a time when it needs blood most. Impaired blood flow produces swelling in the muscle tissue, putting further pressure on nerves and vessels. The result is a vicious cycle of pain, spasm, inflammation, and swelling.

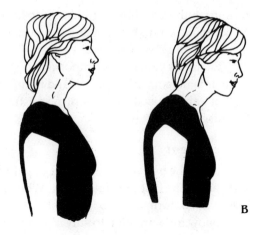

Figure 4-1
Neck posture. **A,** Proper.
B, Improper.

A   B

Prevention of Neck Problems

The best way to treat muscle spasm is to prevent it. This involves maintaining good posture, building balanced strength of your neck muscles, and maintaining flexibility of the ligaments and joints of your neck.

The ideal posture is the so-called flat neck position in which your chin is in and your neck is held up and back. It is important to maintain this posture whether you are standing or sitting (Figure 4-1). Neck spasms can occur while you sleep at night, so it is important to maintain good posture even in bed. It is best not to sleep on your stomach. If you sleep on your side, try to keep a pillow under your neck to maintain a neutral position. Keep your arms down. If you sleep on your back, a 3- to 4-inch pillow should be placed under your neck rather than under your head.

In addition to good posture, it is important to avoid excessive or abrupt motions of your head. In normal daily activities muscle spasms are most likely to result from excessive extension of the neck, as in looking upward. For example, you should not attempt to reach for heavy objects by lifting your hands over your head and looking upward; instead, get a stool or step ladder high enough so that the object is level with your eyes. Similarly, when you play tennis, try to keep your strokes smooth and fluid. Get your entire body into position early so that you can avoid sudden, jerky stretching motions. This is especially true on the serve and overhead shots, even though your ground strokes can cause trouble. With your backhand it is even more important because, when you initiate the backhand stroke, your head is turning forward to the net while your shoulder and arm are moving in the opposite direction as you start your backswing.

Exercises can also be important in preventing neck problems by maintaining muscle strength and tissue flexibility. The same exercises that can be used to prevent neck strain can also be used to treat muscle spasms.

Treatment

What is the best treatment for neck pain caused by muscle spasms or strains? The first principle is rest. When a muscle is acutely stretched, inflamed, torn, or in spasm, it should be rested as much as possible to allow inflammation to subside and healing to begin. In the case of mild neck strains or spasms this can be accomplished simply by taking a few days away from tennis or other vigorous physical activities. In more severe cases it may be advisable to immobilize the neck as well. This can be done with a cervical collar, which can be prescribed by your doctor, purchased at surgical supply houses, or even rigged up yourself by rolling a large bath towel into a tube, wrapping it loosely around your neck, and pinning it. Although a homemade collar may suffice for mild problems, we would advise a carefully measured and fitted collar if more prolonged use seems likely. Foam collars are usually more comfortable than rigid plastic types. A collar should hold your neck in a neutral position without forcing it backward.

When should you wear a collar? The basic principle is to wear it early after the injury, but for only a relatively short time. In the first few days after an injury it may be necessary to wear the collar around the clock. You should quickly try to wean yourself from the collar, perhaps by cutting down on the daytime usage while still wearing the collar at night. The goal is to be independent of the collar within 7 to 10 days.

You can help attain this goal by the use of other treatment modalities. Early after an injury the application of ice packs to your painful neck muscles may help prevent swelling, inflammation, and pain. After the first day or two, however, heat is more helpful to relax muscles, especially before exercise. Medications that fight both pain and inflammation are also extremely helpful and should be used early and often. Buffered aspirin is our favorite; other medications that fight pain and inflammation are described in Chapter 13. Finally, medications that relax muscles and diminish spasm can also be valuable. We generally reserve these medications for cases in which aspirin, heat, and rest are not doing the job. You can also find out more about these medications in Chapter 13.

If all these measures fail to resolve your neck pain, you should see your doctor for a thorough evaluation, including a careful examination to look for signs of pressure on a nerve. In most cases, neck x-ray films should be obtained as well. These tests will help your doctor be sure that you don't have arthritis of the neck, a ruptured cervical intervertebral disc, or nerve compression. If any of these problems exist, or if simple spasms or strains are refractory to usual treatments, your doctor may prescribe cervical traction. Usually this can be accomplished at home, but in the occasional severe case the patient may have to be admitted to the hospital for a brief period of traction.

Rehabilitation

It is not necessary to dwell on the more serious problems because, fortunately, they are uncommon. Most tennis players will find that a short period of rest, heat, and aspirin will relieve their neck spasms and pain. After that it is extremely important to begin a series of exercises to rehabilitate the neck muscles. These exercises will assist in recovery from the acute injury and hopefully will prevent recurrences.

First, we must stress that early on the only "exercise" that is permissible is rest. After the acute pain has settled down, however, you should begin moving your neck. We suggest that you do these exercises while standing in a warm shower so that you will have the benefit of heat. For the first few days the only exercise that you should do is to gently rotate your head to the left and to the right. Move your head slowly and gently toward each side, going only as far as you are comfortable. Try to hold your head at the position of greatest rotation for 5 to 10 seconds before returning it to a central position (Figure 4-2). When your neck is better, you can start flexion and extension exercises. These too can be done in the shower. This is simply a matter of bending your head downward to look at your toes and trying to touch your chin to your chest, and then raising your head upward to look at the ceiling. Again, all motion should be slow and steady. Another helpful exercise is to try to touch your ear to your shoulder. You should keep your head in a central position so that your eyes are looking forward. Don't cheat by shrugging your shoulders; the object is to bring your ear down to your shoulder so that your neck is stretched laterally. Another exercise is to raise both your shoulders to bring them as close as possible to your ears for a

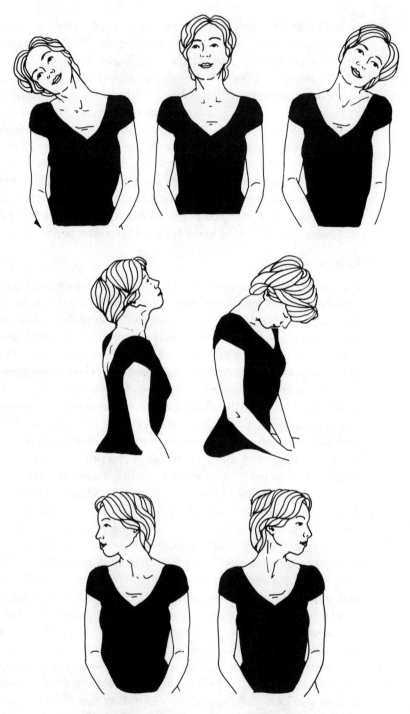

Figure 4-2   Exercises for neck muscle strain.

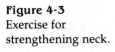

Figure 4-3
Exercise for
strengthening neck.

count of 5, relax, and then stretch your shoulders backward as far
back as possible for another count of 5.

This gentle series of exercises should be done two or three times
a day in a warm shower. When you can accomplish all this and
even play tennis without pain, you can start more strenuous exer-
count of 5, relax, and then stretch your shoulders backward as far
back as possible for another count of 5.

This gentle series of exercises should be done two or three times
a day in a warm shower. When you can accomplish all this and
even play tennis without pain, you can start more strenuous exercises to really build up your neck muscles. Isometric exercises can
be accomplished by thrusting your head forward, backward, or to
the side against the counterpressure of your clasped hands. Hold
the position for 7 seconds without moving your neck, rest for 3
seconds, and then repeat. Build up to a total of 10 repetitions in
each of the four directions. Isotonic exercises can be accomplished
by lying on your stomach with your hands clasped behind your
back (Figure 4-3). With your shoulders back, lift your chin off the
ground as far as possible so that your head rises up from the floor
and tilts back. Try to hold this position for 2 or 3 seconds, and
then relax. Repeat this exercise 5 to 10 times daily. Doing sit-ups
with your knees flexed and your hands clasped behind your neck
may also help strengthen the neck, although this maneuver is
designed principally for the abdominal muscles.

Other Neck Problems

Although muscle sprains, strains, and spasms are the most common
causes of neck pain in tennis players, other problems can occur. This
is particularly true for older players, who may have arthritis of the
spine or disc disease. However, just because you are a senior citizen
doesn't mean that neck pain is due to one of these more serious
problems. With advancing age, muscles become weaker and ligaments

tend to be less supple and elastic, so spasms and strains are more common in older players as well.

Arthritis of the spine can be diagnosed with an x-ray examination. However, x-ray films themselves are not a reliable guide to the degree of pain and disability. For instance, some people are found to have advanced arthritis by x-ray examination but are still able to play tennis without pain or medication. On the other hand, in some people relatively mild degrees of arthritis can produce rather substantial pain. Your doctor will suggest the best way to treat arthritis of your cervical spine. In most cases this involves aspirin or other antiinflammatory medications and a period of rest followed by progressive mobilization and exercises for strength and flexibility. In most cases you should be able to return to the tennis court.

Viral infections can cause muscle inflammation, or myositis. This is a very painful condition but is not serious. The treatment program is similar to the one we use for neck sprains and spasms.

Cervical disc disease is a less common but more serious cause of neck pain. This is less common in the neck than in the lower back, but in both regions the problem is similar. Discs become hardened or inelastic, producing stiffness, immobility, and a deep boring pain. If the disc ruptures or swells outward, it can put pressure on a nerve. In the case of a neck disc, this will produce lightning-like pains or tingling sensations in the arms or hands. It is important to detect this problem because, if it is left unchecked, nerve damage can occur, producing numbness or weakness. All disc problems require individual medical attention. If a conservative regimen of rest (often with a collar or traction), antiinflammatory drugs, and muscle relaxants does not work, a delicate x-ray test called myelography and perhaps even surgery may be necessary.

Neck problems in tennis players can be quite subtle and can masquerade as other ailments. Earlier in this chapter we mentioned that headaches can be caused by excessive tension of the neck muscles. In addition, neck injuries may first appear as pain or stiffness in the shoulder. Because the nerves and blood vessels that supply your arm originate in and pass through the neck, neck injuries can be manifested as arm or even hand pain.

All this sounds complicated and may even seem frightening, but don't let it throw you. With the simple hints for good posture and exercise for strength and flexibility that we have outlined, you should be able to play all the tennis you want without endangering your neck.

5 Shoulder, Arm, and Chest and Lung Problems

The Shoulder

Anatomy and Function

The shoulder joint is an example of an evolutionary trade-off. Originally a strong ball-and-socket joint with a somewhat limited range of motion, it has become one of the most mobile joints of the body; but in exchange the shoulder also has become more lax and much more susceptible to injury.

Your shoulder comprises three bones: the humerus (or arm), the clavicle (collarbone), and the upper and outer portions of the scapula (shoulder blade). The whole apparatus is held together by the shoulder capsule. In addition, the muscles surrounding the shoulder provide a very important layer of support. The combination of ligaments, muscles, and bones gives the shoulder enormous mobility and range of motion, allowing extraordinary maneuvers such as a twist serve and an effective backhand.

The health and stability of the shoulder joint depend on ligaments and muscles. Therefore the best way to prevent injury is a program of strength and flexibility exercises such as those illustrated in Chapters 2 and 3. However, even for a player in the best condition, injuries and pain may occur. Bjorn Borg got through the first three rounds of the 1977 U.S. Open despite a painful right shoulder, but when Dick Stockton (no stranger to injury himself) hit lob after lob in their fourth round match, Borg was simply unable to pivot his shoulder to hit overheads. The result was a forfeit.

Furthermore, as the age of players who are active increases and as players add hours of practice, especially working on their serves, the potential for overuse injuries increases. In the next section of this

Figure 5-1 Supraspinatus tendinitis is associated with tenderness over the anterior part of the shoulder, as shown, or pain if you raise your arm between 45 and 120 degrees to the side.

chapter we will review the more common problems that can affect your shoulder.

Common Shoulder Problems

Tennis shoulder. Tennis shoulder is a drooped posture, with the shoulder on the racquet side lower than the other shoulder. It is due to stretching of the larger muscles and the capsule of the shoulder. It can also be seen in baseball pitchers and other athletes whose sports require a great deal of shoulder motion. Tennis shoulder is painless and requires no treatment, other than the attention of your tailor.

Painful shoulder syndrome. Pain in the shoulder is something else again. It is almost always associated with overuse, which often

A

B

Figure 5-2 Range-of-motion exercises. **A,** Pendulum exercise. Bend over at the waist, supporting yourself with one hand, and allow the other arm to swing like a pendulum with elbow straight. Use a 1- to 2-pound weight. Gradually increase the range of motion. **B,** Wall climbing exercises. Walk your fingers up the wall as far as possible. Go a little higher each day.

means too much, too soon. For example, shoulder pain is all too common after a winter's layoff. Overhead strokes, particularly serves, are especially likely to cause shoulder pain. In addition, shoulder problems seem to be more common in older players.

Shoulder pain often begins as tendinitis, or inflammation in the tendon of the supraspinatus muscle, one of the muscles of the front of the shoulder. Typically, your arm will hurt if you press on your shoulder or if you raise your arm sideway between 45 and 120 degrees (Figure 5-1). This tendon suffers from a suboptimum blood supply and may fray and degenerate with advancing age.

One of the theories advanced to explain the cause of this type of pain and tendinitis is the *impingement syndrome*. The supraspinatus tendon passes underneath an arch of ligaments and is susceptible to being pinched slightly during a serve. Overuse, inflammation, and impingement occur in a vicious cycle, leading to tendinitis and disability.

Treatment and rehabilitation. Because tendinitis seems to be the earliest form of shoulder disability and can lead to a variety of more serious problems, proper treatment at this first stage is important. The principles are the same as for any tendinitis. The degree of *rest* should be proportionate to the degree of discomfort. For minor pain, avoid forceful serves and overhead slams, although you can still hit; if you have severe pain, you may have to take time off from tennis. *Ice* can perform wonders in hastening recovery. Use an ice pack for 5 to 10 minues after you play. If you are benched, use a hot pack followed by cold twice a day. *Antiinflammatory medication,* such as aspirin, has a particularly important role, since the inflammation and swelling may be a major factor in the impingement syndrome and lead to continued pain.

Rehabilitation and prevention are the next steps when your arm can move without too much pain. Range-of-motion exercise such as those in Figure 5-2 can actually be done even if some pain is still present. These include pendulum exercises (allowing your arm to swing like a pendulum while you are bent over) (Figure 5-2, *A*) and wall climbing exercises (walking your fingers up a wall in front of you as far as possible) (Figure 5-2, *B*). As your pain diminishes, you will be able to do these exercises through a progressively wider range of motion and to the side as well.

Flexibility exercises should be added soon afterward (Figure 5-3). Reach your arms behind your back, one over your shoulder, one under, and try to touch your fingers together. The underarm position will cause some discomfort if you have tendinitis, and you may need to help it along with a towel. More advanced flexibility routines are described in Chapter 3.

Strength should be worked on in a similar, progressive manner. While you have pain, do *isometric* exercises in three directions: (1) to the side, pressing against a door jamb or the arms of a chair, (2) forward, pushing your fist against a desk or table, and (3) backward, pushing your elbows against the back of a chair. Each contraction should be held for a count of 7 with a 3-second rest before repeating. Do a set of 10 repetitions in each direction at each daily session.

As the pain diminishes, you can do windmill calisthenics and arm lifts without weights. Finally, begin to use weights or resistance

Figure 5-3
Flexibility exercises.

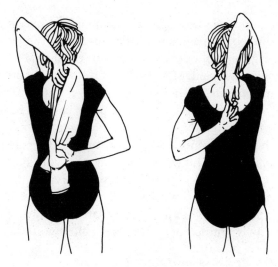

Figure 5-4
Strength exercises.

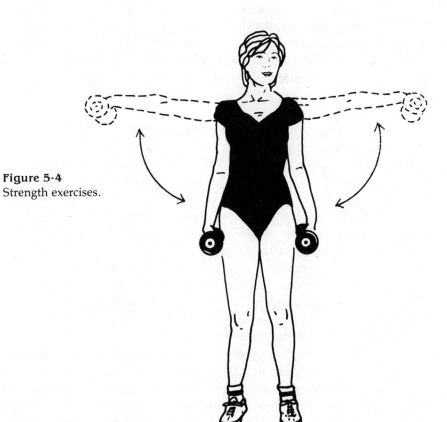

equipment to strengthen your shoulder muscles. Begin with 2-pound dumbbells, paying particular attention to anterior and lateral arm lifts (Figure 5-4), but be careful with the lateral lifts; avoid them if they still cause pain. Move on to the full set of shoulder exercises described in Chapter 2 to help restore your shoulder strength to normal.

When you no longer have pain, you can begin to serve again. As with tennis elbow, your pro may help you more than your doctor at this point, since bad form is one of the major causes of shoulder pain. If you hit the ball too far over your head (either because of a poor toss or trying to hit a twist service), the arc your arm travels may cause the impingement syndrome. Practice your toss, and have a pro watch your form. If you are starting a new type of serve, start slowly with plenty of practice before you use it in a match.

Other Causes of Shoulder Pain

Calcific tendinitis. Repeated injuries and tendinitis may lead to a condition known as calcific tendinitis in which calcium deposits have developed at the site of the tendinitis, as they tend to do at sites of chronic inflammation. These deposits may cause pain because of impingement of the thickened, swollen tendon. Although this condition often improves with the conservative therapy discussed previously, it may require cortisone injections. Rarely, surgery is necessary to remove the calcium deposits.

Bursitis. Another cause of shoulder pain is bursitis. Tendinitis hurts when you move your shoulder; bursitis hurts all the time and is painful enough that you will want to get medical attention. Bursal sacs function by producing lubrication for tendon motion. If they are inflamed, tendons slide with difficulty, compounding the discomfort.

Frequently the question of steroid injections arises in any of the painful shoulder syndromes. If the pain is associated with true bursitis, an injection of steroid medication is not harmful and may produce dramatic relief when other measures have failed. However, an injection into a tendon may lead to atrophy and weakening of the tendon and future problems. Thus the decision depends on the degree to which the problem can be defined and the skill of the physician. It is best done by a specialist.

Frozen shoulder. Severe forms of shoulder pain may require immobilization of your arm for 24 to 48 hours in a sling, but try not to prolong complete rest so that you can avoid developing frozen shoulder. The frozen shoulder is a poorly understood syndrome that can be provoked by injuries of the sort discussed here. It appears to involve inflammation and thickening of the capsule of the shoulder joint itself with resultant loss of motion. It often goes away after a number of months, even without treatment, but mobilization and strengthening exercises seem to hasten recovery in most people. These exercises should be supervised by a professional, since vigorous activity during the acute stage may aggravate the condition. Rarely, mobilization of the joint while under anesthesia may be required.

The use of ice and medication discussed earlier is indicated for all of these more severe types of disability as well. As promptly as possible, pendulum exercises should be initiated, done with the upper body flexed and supported as shown in Figure 5-2. This exercise relaxes the muscle spasm that often accompanies these injuries and allows good pain-free mobilization of the joint. Carrying a light weight (1 or 2 pounds) while doing this exercise helps, but heavier weights tend to require contraction of the shoulder muscles and should be avoided until pain is less and good motion is possible. You should also do flexibility exercises designed to increase your range of motion (see Figure 5-3).

Rotator cuff rupture. Finally, a few conditions are not caused by tennis but frequently affect tennis players. One of the more serious conditions involves the rupture of the *rotator cuff muscles,* the muscles over the front of the shoulder. This problem is characterized by an inability to hold your arm away from your side at a 90-degree angle. This may come from a traumatic injury such as a blow to the shoulder. If the rupture is complete, it may require surgical treatment. However, most are only partial tears and recover with rest followed by exercises. The rehabilitation from surgery also requires a comprehensive set of exercises for strength, joint mobilization, and flexibility. These are best done under the supervision of a physical therapist. Ultrasound may also be helpful. Avoid even practicing serves until most of your strength and range of motion is restored. When you begin to serve again, build up the number of serves slowly. Don't hit full-power serves until your motion and strength have returned.

Dislocation. Another serious condition rarely caused by tennis per se involves dislocation of the shoulder. If you have had two or more dislocations, tennis can precipitate repeated episodes. The most common dislocation occurs when the humerus (arm bone) is displaced forward and downward from its shallow socket. As noted earlier, the shoulder joint depends on ligaments and muscles for its stability. Once a dislocation has occurred, these ligaments are disrupted and there is a high probability of the dislocation recurring. After two dislocations the condition is considered chronic because the integrity of the ligaments has been compromised and the wrong motion will throw it out again. The typical motion causing recurrence is that of swinging the arm up, out, and back, as in putting your arm over the back of a chair or winding up to serve.

Relocation (reduction) should be done by an expert as promptly as possible before muscle spasm and pain appear. Afterward, you'll need to rest your arm in a sling for 3 weeks to allow healing. Finally, a regimen of strength and flexibility exercises is needed for rehabilitation.

However, if you have recurrent dislocatons, your shoulder will dislocate progressively more easily, and tennis serves will become impossible. At that point a decision has to be made regarding surgery to restore the ligamentous structures of the shoulder. Since this is a condition of younger rather than older players, good healing and rehabilitation can be expected following surgery.

Arm Pain

Biceps Tendinitis

A type of tendinitis that may coexist with shoulder tendinitis or may appear on its own is inflammation of the long tendon of the biceps muscle, or biceps tendinitis. Pain from biceps tendinitis is often felt in the front of the upper arm but can also radiate down into the arm and forearm.

Biceps Rupture

Another condition associated with the biceps is rupture of the long head of the biceps muscle. Usually a rupture occurs at the junction between the tendon and muscle at the time of a forceful contraction. There is immediate pain and tenderness, which will then resolve over a few days. The hallmark of this condition is that the muscle will roll up along the front of the arm, producing a prominent bulge instead of a smooth contour. It can be operated on, but few surgeons would do so, since even if it is not repaired, reasonably good function (and thus good tennis) can be maintained.

Occasionally players will notice that their shoulder "snaps" with the service. This condition is a result of the biceps tendon slipping out of its groove. The condition requires no treatment if it is not associated with pain, but if pain is a regular feature, it may require surgical correction.

Back-scratch Bursitis

A syndrome of pain underneath the shoulder blade, or scapula, so-called back-scratch bursitis, has been recently described. It seems to occur because the scapula is jammed against the ribs during the back-scratch portion of the service. Changing your motion is probably the best way to avoid chronic problems with this condition.

Chest and Lung Problems

We have included chest problems in the same chapter as the shoulder and upper arm because the shoulder, upper arm, upper back, and torso all work together in generating smooth, powerful tennis strokes. Aside from back-scratch bursitis and side stitches, muscular chest wall problems are uncommon in tennis players. Internal chest problems are not caused by tennis per se, but heart and lung problems merit discussion because they can be serious. We will comment on lung problems here and heart problems in Chapter 16.

Side Stitches

A stitch in your side—a sudden sharp knifelike pain in your upper abdomen or lower chest—can cost you a point or even a match. Side stitches come on without warning when you are running hard, usually after a series of fast points that have kept you on the move. Although a side stitch will last only a minute or two, the pain can be severe enough to throw off your stride and your timing; in some cases the discomfort may even pull you up short.

Although side stitches are common in tennis players and other athletes, doctors are really not sure what causes the pain. In all likelihood the cause is a muscle cramp or spasm, but there is some controversy as to which muscles are involved. Possibilities include abdominal muscles, the intercostal muscles (small muscles between the ribs, which are responsible for moving your chest wall while you breathe), or the diaphragm (the large muscle between the chest and the abdomen, which is responsible for much of the work of breathing).

What can you do if you get side stitch? Fortunately, the pain will go away when you stop running, so a short breather between points may do the trick. But when you start running again, the pain may recur. Some players find that they can get rid of the pain by bearing down while holding their breath briefly. Doctors call this the *Valsalva maneuver.* If this does not work, you may try pinching your shoulder on the same side as the pain. This sounds like witchcraft but it has a physiologic basis, since the same nerve segment that supplies the diaphragm also goes to the tip of the shoulder.

Of course, the best treatment for side stitches is to prevent them in the first place. As with other muscle cramps, the best protection is to get yourself into top shape with a good conditioning program and to warm up gradually before starting competitive play. In particular, we have found that sit-ups will build abdominal muscle strength and that this helps to prevent side stitches. The best way to do sit-ups is with your knees bent (see Figure 2-13); if necessary, you can hook your feet under a chair or barbell or have a friend hold them down. If your abdominal muscles are weak, start with just a few sit-ups each day, but build up gradually to 20 to 30 sit-ups three or four times a week.

Whereas side stitches are harmless, other types of chest pain can be serious indeed. Of particular concern is heart pain, or angina pectoris. These issues are discussed in detail in Chapter 16.

Breathing Difficulties

Shortness of breath. Do not become alarmed if you become short of breath on the tennis court. Virtually all players will be normally short of breath during at least part of their game. This normal shortness of breath occurs in two forms. The first happens early in the game, especially if you have not warmed up properly. When your game gets into high gear, your muscles have a greatly increased need for oxygen and blood. It takes longer for your heart and lungs to crank up with the rest of your body and you get your "second wind." Although this early shortness of breath is normal and transient, it can hamper your first few points. You can minimize it by conditioning and warm-up routines.

The second type of normal shortness of breath occurs when you are running all out. During maximum exertion your muscles use up more oxygen and build up acid metabolites. In technical terms, your respiratory rate rises as you cross the *anaerobic threshold*. In everyday terms, you feel winded. When you stop running, you will recover your breath and no harm will be done—no harm to your body, that is. Your game is another matter; it can be harmed if your opponent has more "wind" than you do. So work out to build up your maximum oxygen uptake for endurance and to raise your anaerobic threshold for speed. In Chapter 1 we discussed these aspects of conditioning for tennis.

Although these kinds of shortness of breath are normal, in other situations this same sensation can be a warning signal, alerting you to a potentially serious problem. Heart disease can cause shortness of breath with or without chest pain. It can be hard to know for certain whether breathing problems are caused by your heart. Heart problems are more common in older players. You should suspect possible heart trouble if the following occurs: if you become short of breath with mild exertion; if you are sweaty, gray, or disproportionately fatigued; or if you get chest pressure or pain along with the shortness of breath. If you have any question about the health of your heart, be sure to see a doctor.

The other major reason for shortness of breath is lung disease. In medical patients many forms of lung disease can cause this, but in active tennis players only respiratory tract infections and asthma are common enough to warrant consideration.

Respiratory tract infections. Respiratory tract infections are extremely common; sad to say, neither exercise nor diet nor vitamins can protect you from these problems. Most upper respiratory tract infections are caused by viruses. When these infections are confined to your nose and throat (the common cold or sniffles) you can play tennis without worry. But in two other circumstances, you should back off. The first is a flulike illness in which respiratory symptoms are accompanied by various combinations of fever, muscle aches, loss of appetite, and fatigue. The chances are good that, if you have this type of illness, you will not feel like playing tennis. But if you are committed to a match, think twice about it. Your play will be poor, and there is at least a chance that you could harm yourself. Although there is no firm evidence that harm will occur in humans, mice with certain systemic viral illnesses who are forced to exercise can develop serious heart inflammation (myocarditis).

The other common respiratory tract infection that can interfere with tennis is *bronchitis*, an infection of the larger air passages leading to the lungs. Coughing is the major symptom of bronchitis; if bacteria (rather than viruses) cause bronchitis, thick phlegm is produced with the cough. Either viral or bacterial bronchitis can decrease your breathing capacity, so we would suggest a rest from tennis until you are better. You should also see your doctor, since bacterial bronchitis should be treated with antibiotics.

Another respiratory tract ailment that can cause shortness of breath on the courts is *asthma*. Some people develop wheezing principally when they exercise. This is a relatively common problem. Like other forms of asthma, the wheezing and shortness of breath in *exercise-induced asthma* are caused by spasms of the muscles in the bronchial tubes. The bronchial tubes narrow, making the passage of air more difficult and producing a wheezing or whistling sound.

Although exercise-induced asthma differs in some respects from the more common problem of allergic asthma, the two conditions often coexist in the same individual. In allergic asthma, wheezing is often triggered by the inhalation of pollen or dust. In exercise-induced asthma, cold temperatures are chiefly responsible for wheezing. Exercise greatly increases the sensitivity to cold, so people with this problem may find it particularly difficult to play tennis in the spring or fall when the temperature is low.

The simplest solution is to avoid the cold—head indoors a bit early. A face mask may be helpful by warming the air before you inhale it, since the critical factor is the temperature of the air reaching the breathing tubes and lungs. But if you find that you wheeze on the courts, you should see your doctor. Many drugs are available to treat asthma, and these may well permit you to play normally. Be sure to ask your doctor about a trial of Cromolyn. This is an inhalation drug that is generally used to help prevent asthma in children. Cromolyn is not as helpful in most adults with ordinary asthma, but it can be very effective in preventing exercise-induced asthma. You may have to try several types to find which medication is best for you. Keep at it; in all but the most extreme cases you should be able to return to a full tennis schedule.

6   Tennis Elbow

Can an area of inflammation about the size of a quarter be painful enough to make you think about giving up tennis? Only if you let it. Although tennis elbow can be extremely painful, you can take steps to overcome it. And if you follow a rehabilitation program diligently, you may actually end up a better player than you were before tennis elbow struck.

You hear more about this ailment than you used to because of the explosive growth of tennis in the past decade. But tennis elbow is neither new nor all that common. Actually, it is as old as the game itself. Tennis was invented in the 1870s, and almost immediately German doctors began writing about tennis elbow. Today there are simply a lot more tennis players and consequently a lot more aching elbows than in the past. Still, the problem afflicts no more than 10% of the tennis-playing population at one time or another.

What Is Tennis Elbow?

Tennis elbow is defined as painful inflammation of the muscles that extend (straighten) the wrist and fingers. In a sense, then, the problem is really one of "tennis forearm," but the pain usually is most intense in the small area where the tendons attach to the elbow, called the *epicondyle*. The outer (or lateral) epicondyle is involved in most cases, although the inner (or medial) epicondyle may sometimes be affected, especially in better players. The pain itself is triggered by inflammation and swelling of the tissues of the epicondyle, but there also may be small tears in the tendon.

Who Gets "The Elbow"?

A 10% chance of getting tennis elbow may seem discouragingly high, but remember two things. First and foremost, tennis elbow can be prevented. If you follow the basic advice we will give you *before* you ever get it, the chances are good that you will be one of the lucky 90% of tennis players who are forever free of elbow pain. The second point to keep in mind is that not all tennis players are equally vulnerable. Although tennis elbow can afflict anyone ranging from beginners to champions such as Manuel Orantes (who required surgery in July 1980) and Tony Roche, certain factors make tennis elbow more likely. Your age is a major factor: tennis elbow is rare in players younger than 20 years and is most frequent between the ages of 35 and 50. In these middle years the body's strength and flexibility begin to decline, yet the enthusiasm of youth has not yet been tempered by the wisdom of maturity. As a result, players overuse their arms, which puts excessive stress on tissues that have begun to lose their resiliency. The result is a pain in the elbow.

Tennis elbow is relatively uncommon in beginners and in occasional players who simply don't hit often enough or hard enough to stress their forearm and elbow. Yet the pros who hit the hardest are also relatively safe because their superior conditioning and excellent stroking techniques protect them from this problem.

Thus you are most likely to suffer from ''the elbow'' if you are a middle-aged player of average or above-average ability who plays two or three times a week. But even nonplayers can get true tennis elbow. In fact, any repetitive use of the elbow and forearm can cause inflammation and pain in the elbow. Usually, this is related to occupational overuse; dentists, baseball pitchers, and carpenters— especially ''do-it-yourselfers''—*all* can get tennis elbow without ever picking up a racquet. We have even seen patients with typical tennis elbow caused by using hair dryers, and after any long election campaign there are always a few cases of ''candidate's elbow'' from all that handshaking.

Causes of Tennis Elbow

Despite all the attention tennis elbow has received, its true cause remains a mystery. Probably there are a number of contributing factors. First is the excessive use of the elbow and forearm. The repetitive nature of tennis strokes is surely a key element.

Another element is force overload. The object of tennis is to apply strong forces to a moving ball at the point of impact, but if your body mechanics, technique, and equipment are not right, you may apply excessive force to your own body tissues instead. Still another factor is the condition of your body. It can be harder to withstand the stresses of tennis if you have weak forearm muscles, muscular imbalance, a lack of flexibility, or poor endurance. Deficiencies in any of the areas can lead to tennis elbow.

Among club players, tennis elbow strikes the outer, or lateral, part of the elbow in about 9 cases out of 10. This injury seems to result most often from mechanically faulty backhand ground strokes. But among the pros the inner, or medial, surface of the elbow is more commonly involved. Unlike club players, they are being penalized, ironically, for good technique. The back-scratch position, an integral part of an excellent serve, places the inner part of the elbow under great stress. Those stresses are further exaggerated on some spin serves, particularly the American twist serve. Because good players take their racquets so far back on their serves and hit with such great spin, they can develop tennis elbow as they grow older. Younger players can usually tolerate those stresses with relatively few problems, but they can have trouble later on; the pros who have had the most severe cases of tennis elbow were usually 30 or older.

The Test for Tennis Elbow

It may be hard for your doctor to diagnose tennis elbow: the x-ray examination is perfectly normal in this condition, and there is no laboratory test for tennis elbow. You should be able to diagnose yourself with a simple maneuver (Figure 6-1). Hold your arm at your side, bend your elbow to 90 degrees, and hold your fingers out parallel to the ground. Have a friend push down on your hand while you try as hard as you can to resist this pressure by lifting your hand up. If you feel pain in the outer part of the elbow, you probably do have tennis elbow. You can confirm this by making a fist and having your friend squeeze your outer elbow—pain and tenderness also suggest that you have ''the elbow.''

To test for medial tennis elbow, hold your arm in the same position and have your friend press up against your palm while you exert downward force. Pain on the inside of your elbow—together with tenderness when your friend squeezes here—strongly suggests that you have the less common, medial variety of tennis elbow.

Even these tests are not infallible. There are many possible causes of elbow pain in tennis players, including bone chips, calcium deposits, bursitis, and arthritis. X-ray examinations can help detect many of these other conditions. If your symptoms are atypical, or if they don't respond to treatment, you should see your doctor to be sure you don't have one of these other problems.

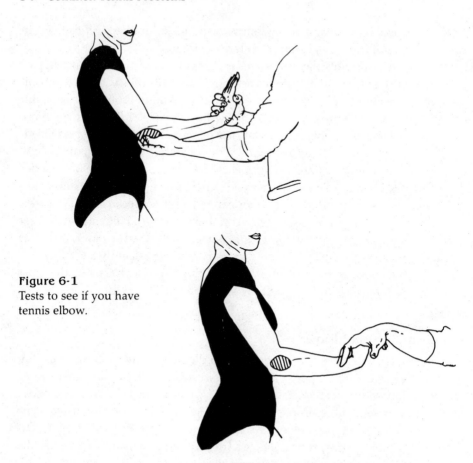

Figure 6-1
Tests to see if you have
tennis elbow.

Treatment of Tennis Elbow

The causes of tennis elbow are diverse, and with treatment, too, there are many approaches, controversies, and unresolved questions. To avoid confusion when you seek advice, keep a few basic rules in mind. First, be suspicious of simple answers and guaranteed cures; there are no magic treatments. Second, be conservative: always start with the simplest treatments, which rely on ice, rest, exercises, equipment, and technique. Use medications only if these programs fail, and reserve steroid injections for a last resort and operations for a last, last resort. Most important, be patient and optimistic. In most cases tennis elbow will resolve completely. It may take 6 months or even longer, but you can expect to play without pain at the end of that time.

If you are one of the thousands of people with true tennis elbow, what can you do to lessen pain and return to play? The first goal is to *reduce inflammation*. If your pain comes on suddenly and is severe, you should elevate your elbow, apply ice, and apply pressure by wrapping your elbow with a snug elastic bandage. In the early stages of the injury you should probably give your arm a rest. If the pain is very severe, you may even want to use an arm sling or a forearm-wrist splint to provide immobilization and support. However, this type of nearly total rest can cause stiffness, weakness, and even muscle atrophy, so get your arm moving as soon as you can. A good compromise is selective rest: use your arm as much as possible but avoid any movement that causes pain. In the case of tennis elbow the painful motions may be quite specific. You may find, for example, that you can continue forehand strokes without difficulty but that you must avoid all backhands. The same selective rest should apply to your daily activities as well.

Although selective avoidance of painful motions is an important tool to combat the pain of tennis elbow, it is not enough. For one thing, you need other ways to fight inflammation. You should apply ice to the inflamed part of your elbow and wrap it loosely with an elastic bandage. You can place small pieces of foam rubber under the bandage at the points of greatest tenderness to increase the pressure gently without excessively constricting your entire elbow.

Rest and ice, though, may not be enough to ease your pain. In that case you should try a medication that reduces inflammation. Aspirin is the simplest and safest one. If this doesn't do the job, your doctor may prescribe drugs such as indomethacin or one of the newer antiinflammatory agents. Be aware that these drugs can have harmful side effects. These medications are discussed further in Chapter 13.

The most powerful antiinflammatory drugs are the steroid hormones such as cortisone and its derivatives. Steroids can be taken in pill form, and they might make your elbow feel better. However, these powerful hormones have many serious side effects, and we feel they should never be used orally for tennis elbow; the benefits simply are not worth the risks.

Steroids also can be injected directly into the inflamed area of your elbow. The side effects of local steroid injections are less, but they can cause weakness of the tendons themselves, which may even lead to rupture of a tendon. So ask your doctor to save steroid injections for a last resort, and don't have more than one or two shots. In most cases conservative treatment will do the trick and steroids will not be necessary. Remember that, even if you get a steroid shot, you will still need to follow the rehabilitation program outlined below.

Even with respect to the less potent antiinflammatory drugs, your goal should be to use medications only when they are needed. When your pain begins to subside, you should stop taking drugs and progress from rest to active rehabilitation. When you return to the court, you may want to take two aspirin tablets 1 hour before you play. This schedule is quite safe and may help prevent recurrent inflammation.

Rehabilitation

The first step in fighting tennis elbow is to reduce inflammation with selective rest, ice, and in some cases antiinflammatory medications. But the next step in your battle is equally important: active rehabilitation. In fact, these exercises are the key to recovery and to the long-range prevention of tennis elbow.

Naturally, you should exercise to improve your strength and flexibility. Although your elbow and forearm are the inflamed areas, your problem may stem from weakness, inflexibility, or muscle imbalance elsewhere in your upper body, and that could be forcing you to overuse your forearm to compensate. Therefore it is important to exercise your entire arm, shoulder, and trunk so that other muscles and joints can take some of the load off your elbow. In fact, you should start with your other muscle groups first, adding elbow and forearm exercises only after the inflammation has subsided.

Do exercises to strengthen and stretch the muscles in your upper arm, shoulder, upper back, and racquet hand, as well as your forearm. Start slowly, and gradually increase your daily repetitions of each exercise. Some helpful exercises are demonstrated in Chapters 2 and 3. The wrist curls (Figure 2-23) are particularly important in rehabilitation from tennis elbow.

Returning to Tennis

Although relief of pain is important to all players with tennis elbow, returning to tennis is even more important. You can and will be able to play again, but don't rush it; some restraints and precautions will actually get you back to full action faster.

When you return to tennis, begin with practice sessions rather than competition. At first hit only forehands. When you are ready to resume all strokes, be sure that you don't push yourself to the point of pain.

Before even going on the court, massage the elbow, rub in a heat-producing liniment, or apply a heating pad to the painful area. Then go through a comprehensive series of upper body stretching exercises and some forearm exercises before you hit a ball. Even though your pain is localized in your elbow, stretch and warm up your shoulder, forearm, and wrist as well so that they can help share the stress of hitting the ball.

When you begin hitting, go at half speed. Your elbow pain should ease after 10 or 15 minutes of gently rallying. When you finish, apply an ice pack to your elbow. A whirlpool or ultrasound treatment may help reduce inflammation after play.

Equipment

Careful attention to equipment may also help overcome tennis elbow. There is no one racquet that is best for all players with tennis elbow. Trial and error may be necessary to find the racquet suited to your game. Your local pro should be able to help.

There are, however, some general guidelines you can follow. Good balance is the first and the most important consideration. Head-light or evenly balanced racquets are preferable to head-heavy ones for tennis elbow sufferers. Next, take care to choose a racquet that has the largest grip size you can comfortably handle. A bigger grip size helps reduce both the amount of torque (twist) a racquet undergoes as it strikes the ball and the amount of strength you need to control the racquet head. Both these factors lessen the stress on your arm.

As construction materials used in racquets continue to evolve and proliferate, it is becoming increasingly difficult to recommend a specific kind of racquet. Some players have found relief by switching from wood to metal, fiberglass, or graphite, whereas others have found the reverse to be true. You may want to experiment with one of the new, larger racquets, which have bigger sweet spots. Theoretically the larger sweet spots of the midsized and oversized racquets should cut down on those stress factors caused by off-center hits.

Don't string your racquet extremely tight unless you have Bjorn Borg's forearm strength (which you probably don't). In a standard-sized racquet, 16-gauge gut strung between 52 and 55 pounds is usually best.

With all this attention to your racquet, it's important not to overlook your tennis balls. Avoid heavy, dead balls, and never play with wet tennis balls. A few extra cans of new balls won't cure tennis elbow, but they may help a little, so indulge yourself at the pro shop.

Even the surface on which you play can make a difference. Slow surfaces such as clay absorb some of the velocity of the oncoming tennis ball, so there will be less force to overcome when it makes contact with your racquet. Even on a fast surface you can get similar protection by slowing down your game. Unless your opponent also has tennis elbow, this is easier said than done—so pick clay if the choice is available.

Another piece of equipment that may help is a forearm support. This is a wide band of adjustable nonelastic fabric designed to be worn just below the elbow. Some players get additional relief by using a support that has a second band just above the wrist. A support should be snug, but not so tight that it interferes with blood flow. If the support causes pain, it is too tight. Loosen your support between games to avoid swelling in your hand, and snug it up again when you resume play. Wear the support only when you are playing.

Stroking Technique

Although tennis elbow is a medical problem, the most important advice for recovery (and prevention) will come not from your doctor but from your teaching pro. Better stroking is perhaps the best way to conquer the problem. A few lessons to improve your technique may be far more beneficial than expensive visits to a doctor's office.

In cases of outer, or lateral, tennis elbow, faulty backhands are usually the culprits. If you hit your backhand by leading with your elbow, you may be asking for trouble. Your goal should be to avoid using your forearm for power while still relying on it for control. Be sure to turn your body sideways to the net, take an early backswing, and meet the ball slightly in front of your body. Keep your front shoulder down and your elbow and wrist firm. Generate power from your shoulder and a smooth forward transfer of your weight; don't make your forearm do all the work. If your problem persists, you may want to consider learning a two-handed backhand. Two-handed players rarely suffer from lateral tennis elbow.

In short, good technique is a key element in your recovery from tennis elbow. Elbow pain should be a signal that you may have faulty stroking mechanics, so use your recovery period to retool your strokes. Go slowly, concentrating on proper form and smooth footwork.

This same advice may save you from getting tennis elbow in the first place. You can prevent tennis elbow by making certain your strokes are technically sound and by exercising to keep your upper body strong and flexible.

Is There a Cure?

Is it possible to recover completely from a bad case of tennis elbow? The answer is a resounding yes. But you must be patient, persistent, and optimistic. In most cases the pain of tennis elbow will diminish substantially or subside entirely within about 6 months. Don't rush to get steroid injections or to undergo surgery. In some cases these treatments can help, but they should be used as a court of last resort only when simpler measures fail to get you back on the court. If you invest a few months in exercises and lessons, beginning slowly and gradually increasing your playing time and power, you can conquer tennis elbow while also improving your game.

7 The Forearm, Wrist, and Hand

The whole object of tennis is to hit the ball with force and accuracy. The power of your tennis swing involves your entire body. The weight of your torso is shifted forward on your hips and legs, and your upper body generates a tremendous amount of force at the shoulder and arm. All this power is transmitted to the racquet through your forearm, wrist, and hand. Obviously the wrist and hand are critical for accurate tennis shots. One might suspect that, because they are the recipients of the full power of your swing, they would be subject to frequent injuries. Happily this is not the case; injuries to the wrist and hand are relatively uncommon in tennis players.

The Forearm

The forearm is composed of two bones, the radius and the ulna. The ulna is largest at the elbow and is a major component of the elbow joint, whereas the radius is larger at the wrist and is a major component of the wrist joint. These two bones are surrounded by groups of muscles that function to extend (bend backward) and flex (bend forward) the wrist. In addition to bending motions at the wrist and elbow, the bones of the forearm can also undergo complex rotary movements, which are important in putting a top spin on your shots.

Strains

Although it is rare for the forearm muscles to be seriously injured in tennis players, they can experience two very different problems. The first of these stems from the weakness of the muscles and is exacerbated by the overuse stresses generated by frequent tennis. The result of weakness and overuse can be strain of the forearm muscles. Although this can produce pain and weakness in the forearm itself, it is often also a leading cause of tennis elbow, as discussed in Chapter 6.

Forearm strains should be treated like any other muscle strain. In severe or acute strains you should avoid playing and rest your arm. In such cases a splint may even be prescribed by your doctor. However, it's important that you avoid prolonged immobilization of your fingers even if your arm is in a splint, since your fingers are likely to stiffen up quickly and finger motion actually puts little stress on the forearm itself. In most cases a splint is not necessary, and you can rest your forearm sufficiently simply by taking some time away from the courts. When you do get back to play, be sure that you warm up adequately before each game. Start off slowly, and don't overdo it. After you play, you can apply ice to your forearm to reduce swelling and inflammation. Aspirin or other antiinflammatory drugs can also help in this regard. Finally, a forearm support is helpful to many players who play with forearm strain (Chapter 6). Wrist exercises that will help rehabilitate you from forearm strain and prevent recurrent problems are given in Chapter 2, especially Figure 2-23.

Hypertrophy

The second major forearm problem is exactly the reverse of weakness and strain. Despite its formidable name, hypertrophy is really not a problem at all, in that it merely reflects the normal enlargement of muscle fibers that are subjected to frequent exercise. Most competitive tennis players note some degree of enlargement of their racquet arm, particularly the forearm, because their muscles are built up through exercise. Far from being an injury, it is actually a sign of muscular strength and requires no treatment.

The Wrist

The wrist is composed of eight small bones, the carpal bones, which are bound together by strong ligaments. The blood vessels and nerves that supply the hand pass over these bones and under some of the ligaments, so they can be damaged by pressure when the wrist itself is injured.

Sprains and Strains

Because proper tennis strokes require a rigid wrist, the wrist itself is generally spared from overuse injuries in tennis, but in some cases a wrist sprain may occur. Although we call this a *sprain,* it is usually actually a strain, since tendons are involved more frequently than ligaments. If your wrist tendons are strained repeatedly, they can become inflamed. This condition is called *tenosynovitis* and can produce pain and swelling at the wrist.

The early treatment for wrist strain is ice, elevation, and rest. Most tennis-related wrist injuries do not require a splint but can be treated with an Ace bandage wrap. A wrist wrap can even be worn during play until your wrist has healed and the pain is gone. Remember to exercise your fingers gently even if the injury is severe enough to require a wrist splint.

Ganglions

Tennis players may also note a variety of other wrist problems. Although these are not actually caused by tennis, they can interfere with your game and thus merit brief discussion.

A frequent wrist problem is the ganglion. This is a painless swelling on the back of the wrist; the cause is unknown, but in some players a ganglion can become painful from overuse of the wrist with chronic strain. Although the ganglion is a common ailment, its exact composition is subject to some debate. In most cases it probably represents a bulging and swelling of the smooth membranes that lie in the wrist joints and surround the tendons. Usually, these synovial sacs are filled with fluid and therefore are soft and movable, but in some cases a ganglion can be quite firm.

If you have a ganglion, your tennis partner may try to help you by slamming the back of your wrist with a heavy book. Unfortunately, these traditional methods of rupturing the sac often fail and the swelling recurs. In fact, even if your doctor removes the fluid by aspirating it into a syringe through a needle, the swelling tends to recur. So we recommend avoiding both of these treatments. You can try the treatment program outlined for wrist strain above. If the ganglion doesn't interfere with your play or daily activities, leave it alone. But if you find that your wrist strength and mobility are adversely affected, you should discuss definitive surgical removal with your doctor.

Carpal Tunnel Syndrome

Another wrist problem that can interfere with tennis is the carpal tunnel syndrome. In this disorder the ligament that runs across the underside of your wrist becomes thickened, putting pressure on the nerves that run down the forearm, across the wrist, and into the hand. There are many possible causes of this condition, but in most cases the actual reason that the ligament becomes thickened is not known. Tennis per se should not cause the problem, but overuse of the wrist may aggravate it.

The earliest symptom of carpal tunnel syndrome is tingling at the tips of the thumb, index finger, and middle finger. At first you will not notice this when you play tennis, but it can be quite annoying during quiet times, especially at night. In advanced cases the pain can become quite severe and can prevent you from gripping your racquet properly.

With mild carpal tunnel syndrome you can continue to play. With a more acute case you may have to rest, possibly immobilizing your wrist with a splint. If this does not do the trick, you may have to consider antiinflammatory medications, which may sometimes include cortisone injections. For persistent or advanced cases, surgical release of the thickened ligament is the definitive form of treatment. Results of the surgery are generally excellent, and you should be able to return to normal tennis.

The Hand

The hand is one of the most complex, intricate, and wonderful parts of the human body. Artists and sculptors go to great lengths to capture the beauty of the hand. Writers and poets also wax eloquent on the subject. Anthropologists produce learned treatises on the importance of the hand in human evolution, and doctors write whole books on the structure and function of this one small part of the human anatomy. But for the tennis player, all of the hand's wondrous complexity is reduced to one task: to hold the racquet firmly.

Beginning tennis players are taught to think of their racquet as an extension of their hand. From a medical point of view just the reverse is true: most hand problems are an extension of racquet problems caused by an improper grip, excessive torque, or both.

Blisters

Blisters of the palm are a good example of the way your grip can affect your hand. The most common causes of blisters are excessive friction, excessive pressure, and excessive moisture. If you are subject to blisters, be sure to dry your racquet hand between each point. It might be useful to experiment with different grip surfaces to find the one that will absorb moisture best while still giving you a firm grip. Some players have found that wrapping the grip handle with gauze is helpful. Another way to keep your hand dry and your grip firm is to use rosin between games. Exercises to strengthen your hand muscles will also help you maintain a firm grip. Similarly, it is important to be certain that your racquet's grip size is correct. If the grip is too small, the racquet may tend to twist in your hand on impact with the ball, causing friction. Finally, if the blisters recur in the same spot, you can protect the skin by applying a Band-Aid before each match. If large areas are involved, a protective glove may prove useful; thin gloves worn by golfers and baseball players are light and flexible enough for tennis. Gradually, with regular play, the skin on your hands will toughen and the problem should disappear.

Cracked Skin

Another cause of hand pain is cracked skin. Although this is a simple problem, it can cause enough discomfort to seriously impair your game. The most common cause of cracked, painful skin is excessive dryness. Dryness of the skin is in fact caused by exposure to water because water removes the oily lubricants that keep your skin moist. Heavy perspiration can cause this, as can repeated hand washing. Try to keep your skin free of moisture by removing the perspiration with a towel between games. Also remember to put the lubricants back into your skin after you wash your hands. A variety of emollient lotions are available to restore moisture, but two of our favorites are Eucerin cream and Keri lotion. If these simple measures don't alleviate symptoms such as cracked, dry skin on your palm, you should see a dermatologist to find if you have some form of dermatitis or eczema; often these can be dramatically helped by medications such as steroid creams.

Strains

The muscles and tendons of the hand can be subject to overuse and strain because of the recurrent trauma of gripping a tennis racquet firmly. Jimmy Connors nearly lost his match with unseeded Andre Gomes in the 1981 U.S. Open because of hand cramps. We are not sure what caused Connors' hand cramps, but such symptoms generally are caused by chronic strain of the intrinsic muscles of the racquet hand. Fatigue and weakness of the hand are early symptoms. Later you may notice pain in your hand whenever you grip your tennis racquet, and eventually you may develop cramps and even muscle spasms. Rest is the main element of treatment, but you may have to get through an important match before you can rest your hand. Connors got relief by dipping his hand in a cooler, and ice packs may be helpful to you as well. In the long run you should try to prevent the problem by building up your hand strength. You can do this by squeezing a small rubber ball or a special hand grip—strengthening device available at sporting goods stores.

Tenosynovitis and Fractures

Persistent pain in the palm can also reflect inflammation of the muscles and tendons that flex your fingers. Like other forms of tenosynovitis, this will generally respond to rest, antiinflammatory medications such as aspirin, and heat. If you have severe and persistent pain, you cannot assume that it is simply caused by inflammation. The repeated impact of the racquet butt on your hand can actually be traumatic enough to fracture one of the small bones of the wrist. This type of fracture most often affects the hamate, a small bone in the wrist at the base of the little finger. The hamate bone has a small projection or hook that can be fractured by the force of your racquet against your hand. If this happens, you will notice severe wrist pain, a weak grip, and tenderness over the fracture site. If there is swelling, the ulnar nerve can be compressed, causing tingling of your little finger. Special x-ray views are needed to diagnose this injury. It's important to discover it early so that it can be treated appropriately. For a small hairline fracture a short-arm cast with a little finger splint will generally do the trick, but for a more severe displaced fracture, surgery may be required.

Nerve Compression

Although a fractured hamate is a serious injury, it is quite uncommon, so don't assume the worst if you have mild hand discomfort. For instance, although tingling in your little finger can follow a fractured hamate, it more often results from simple compression of the ulnar nerve as it runs along the palm to the little finger. If your grip is too tight, you can compress the nerve, which will cause tingling but no lasting damage. Backboard play is more likely to bring this because of the fast action, which requires a tight grip for prolonged periods. This type of simple traumatic nerve compression is not serious but can be annoying. To relieve it, be certain your racquet is the right size for your hand. Above all, loosen your grasp as often as you can, even if it means pausing at the backboard or supporting the weight of your racquet with your other hand between points.

The Fingers

Injuries

Many hand problems of tennis players involve the palm, but finger injuries can occur in some cases. Many players develop large calluses at the base of the thumb after years of frequent play, but this does not ordinarily produce discomfort or disability. However, repeated trauma to the tendons that flex the fingers can produce inflammation and swelling, and if this continues unchecked, there can be actual restriction of the gliding motion of the tendons within their smooth sheaths. The result is called *trigger finger.* In its mildest form a trigger finger merely produces a snapping sensation when you make a fist. In some cases motion of the finger can be impaired, and the finger may even lock completely. Rest, heat, and antiinflammatory medications may suffice for mild cases. Steroid injections and splinting may be helpful for moderately severe cases, but surgery is the only way to correct an advanced case of trigger finger well enough to allow you to hold your racquet properly.

Infections

Infections of your fingers can also hamper your style. The most common infection is paronychia. This process starts at the rim of the nail but can spread to involve your entire fingertip. Your finger will be warm, swollen, red, and painful. Greenish discoloration or pus may also be evident. You should avoid traumatizing the area, so you may have to take a few days away from the courts until you're better. The cornerstone of treatment is to soak your finger in warm water with a pinch of salt for 20 minutes, four times daily. If you fail to improve, if you have a fever, or if you notice red streaks on your finger, see your doctor at once to get antibiotics directed against the staphylococcal bacteria that is causing the problem. Nail surgery may be needed in some cases.

Your Grip

By far the most important way to keep your hand healthy during tennis is to pay attention to your racquet size and to your grip. When you began tennis lessons, the first thing you did was to shake hands with your instructor, and the next was to shake hands with your racquet. Unfortunately, very little attention is given to grip

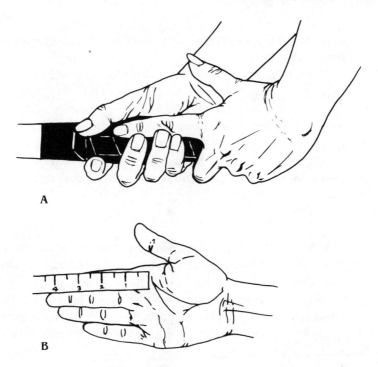

Figure 7-1   Grip size is one of the most important considerations in selecting a racquet. We advocate the "Goldilocks rule": Pick a grip that is not too big, not too small, but just right for you. Trial and error is the ultimate test, but at today's racquet prices you need a good way to predict which size will be best. **A,** The "rule of finger." Hold your racquet in the eastern grip. Your thumb and index finger should almost touch. The index finger of your other hand should be able to fit snugly between your fingertips and the base of your thumb. A loose fit indicates a racquet size that is too big; a very tight fit tells you the racquet is too small. **B,** Palm measurement method. Measure the distance in inches from the tip of your ring finger to the lower horizontal crease in your palm to get the proper grip size. Since most racquets are available in only ⅛-inch increments (4⅜, 4½, 4⅝, etc.), if your hand falls between two sizes, pick the larger size to help prevent tennis elbow.

selection and technique after the first few lessons. If you are having problems with your hand (or with your shot control), review your grip technique with your instructor or pro. Your choice of eastern, western, or continental gripping techniques should be settled by you and your coach, not your doctor. Pay careful attention to the fine points of whatever grip you select. Your ball control will improve, and you will have fewer visits to your doctor for hand and forearm problems.

Racquet size is also very important. Maximum velocity and control require a tight grip, but if the racquet butt is too big, your hand will tire and you will be unable to maintain a good grip. A racquet that is too small is no better; the racquet will tend to twist in your hand, creating more torque at the expense of ball control. Figure 7-1 shows how to measure your hand to determine the racquet grip size that is best for you. If you have any doubt, check with your pro.

• • •

Although hand injuries are relatively uncommon in tennis players, they can be serious and even disabling. Your hand is a marvelously complex and efficient structure, but to function optimally, all its parts must be just right. Treat it with respect. Even seemingly minor hand injuries can lead to important complications if they are not treated properly. Because of this, we generally advise that players seek medical attention for hand injuries earlier than they might for similar injuries to other parts of the body.

8   The Abdomen, Hip, and Thigh

From an anatomic point of view, the muscles, ligaments, joints, and bones of your abdomen, pelvis, hip, and thigh are quite distinct from each other. However, from a functional point of view, these structures are intimately interrelated. During both tennis and ordinary daily activities these parts of your body work together to maintain an erect posture, to transfer weight from your trunk to your legs, and to propel your body forward (or backward) through motion at the hip. Because of this close interaction, it is not surprising that an injury to one region frequently causes secondary problems in adjacent structures. In addition, when injury occurs to one of these tissues, the pain is often referred to a second area, sometimes producing diagnostic confusion. For all these reasons we will consider the abdomen, hip, and thigh together in this chapter.

Abdominal Strains or Muscle Pulls

Many tennis players tend to have underdeveloped abdominal muscles. A potbelly is bad enough, but weak abdominal muscles also cause tennis injuries. Weakness of your abdomen may put extra stress on your back and can contribute to lower back problems. In addition, your abdominal muscles themselves can be injured during tennis. This is most likely to occur when your muscles are subjected to sudden stretching motions, as in reaching for an overhead or service shot.

You will know you have a pulled abdominal muscle because you will get a steady pain over the injured muscle during and after exercise. A pulled abdominal muscle is different from a side stitch; although a side stitch is very painful during exercise, the

109

pain is quickly relieved by rest and usually won't come back even if you start playing again. This difference between a simple stitch and a muscle pull is explained by the underlying problem. A stitch is caused by a spasm or cramp in the muscle. In contrast, an abdominal pull is actually a strain of the large rectus abdominus muscle. As in other muscle strains, there is tearing of the muscle fibers in this type of injury. In mild strains only a few fibers are torn and the pain is not accompanied by any loss of strength. However, on some occasions the tear may involve more fibers, which results in weakness of the muscle.

The pain caused by an abdominal muscle strain can sometimes be confused with pain caused by diseases of the internal organs such as the appendix, intestines, and urinary tract. Sometimes your physician may order an x-ray examination or tests to check your internal organs, but you can save yourself a lot of time and money by first doing a simple test for an abdominal muscle strain. Lie on your back on a firm surface; tense your abdomen by raising your head and legs simultaneously or by raising your legs against resistance. If this test causes the same pain, it is likely that you have a strained abdominal muscle rather than a potentially more serious problem with an internal organ. If you have fever, altered intestinal function, or severe abdominal pain, you should see your doctor.

Treatment

The treatment of an abdominal muscle pull is similar to that of other muscle strains. Ice is helpful for the early treatment of these injuries. Later in the rehabilitation of an acute strain or in the case of a chronic strain, heat may actually be more helpful. Similarly, rest is important at first, but as healing occurs, progressively more exercise can be allowed. A mild strain need not interrupt your tennis, but if you have a more severe injury, it is prudent to stay off the courts until the pain is significantly diminished; otherwise you can reinjure your abdominal muscles and end up losing even more court time.

Rehabilitation

Prevention and rehabilitation involve strengthening your abdominal muscles. This is best accomplished by doing sit-ups. However, you should not attempt the traditional marine recruit regimen of 100 sit-ups with your knees out straight and your hands behind your head. This program has two important errors. First, you should always do sit-ups with your knees bent. Second, you should start gradually and add repetitions slowly. At first you may not be able to do more than 5 to 10 sit-ups per day. You can increase the number by two or three every third day as you feel your strength building up. At first you can keep your hands at your side; when you are stronger, switch to a position in which your hands are clasped behind your neck. Finally, as your strength peaks, you can begin your sit-ups with your legs out straight and bring your knees up at the same time as you raise your trunk. Eventually you should be able to do 30 to 50 sit-ups in about 3 minutes. It is not necessary to do them every day, but three or four workouts per week will keep your abdominal muscles in shape. The grunting and sweating will be worthwhile; you will protect your abdominal muscles from strain injuries, you will improve your posture and protect your back, and your flat abdomen will look better as well.

The Pelvis

Your pelvis is a circle of strong bones and ligaments that serves to transfer weight from the single axis of your trunk to your two legs. The strong bones also protect your internal pelvic organs. The sacroiliac joints at the rear of the pelvis can produce lower back pain in tennis players. Aside from this, pelvic injuries are uncommon in tennis, since pelvic injuries are generally produced by direct trauma, such as the deep bruise or "hip pointer" from football or other contact sports. Hopefully, the only contact in tennis is between your racquet and the ball, so your pelvic bones should be free of problems.

However, an occasional player may develop pelvic pain. In some cases this will be referred pain from the internal organs of the intestinal or genitourinary tract. In other cases back problems may masquerade as pelvic pain. On occasion the repeated trauma of running on a hard court surface may produce a small stress fracture in the pelvic bones of frequent, intense players. This can happen either near the sacroiliac joint or at the front part of the pelvis, the pubic symphysis. As in other stress fractures, x-ray films may not show the injury for as long as 3 to 4 weeks. In contrast, a bone scan can diagnose the problem earlier. The only treatment is rest. Once the pain has diminished, you should be able to return to the courts without problems. To prevent recurrences, return to play gradually, build up slowly, select shoes that will cushion and absorb shock, and play on a soft surface such as clay or grass whenever possible.

The Hips

Your hips are obviously among the most important joints in your body. Despite this, the hip is often misunderstood. Chances are that, if we asked you to put your hands on your hips, you would settle your hands comfortably at your waist. Your hands would be resting on the bony prominences of your pelvis (the iliac crest) and in fact would be nowhere near your hip joints, which are about 6 inches lower down.

The hip is a ball-and-socket joint. The socket is formed by the pelvic bones, whereas the ball is the head of the thigh bone, or femur. Strong ligaments help keep the ball of the thigh bone in the socket of the pelvis, but the ligaments themselves don't really prevent abnormal motion. Instead, the very strong muscles that surround the hip are principally responsible for stabilizing the joint while allowing normal mobility.

Strains

Because of the great mobility of the hip joint, sprain injuries of the ligaments are uncommon. However, the muscles and tendons can be strained, either by a sudden violent stress or by chronic overuse. Hip muscle strain will show up as deep discomfort in your buttock or hip when you play tennis, with slow relief as you rest off the court. As with other muscle strains, the treatment includes early ice and rest, with progressive exercise, heat, and antiinflammatory drugs such as aspirin later on.

Bursitis

Although we often speak of hip bursitis as a single entity, there are actually 13 different bursal structures in the hip area. The most common type of hip bursitis involves an inflammation of the bursa over the outside portion of the hip, the greater trochanter. This is the bony prominence of the thigh bone, which you can feel at the outside of your hip joint. If you have bursitis in this region, it will be tender to the touch. You can get relief by applying ice immediately after you play and switching over to heat after a day or two. Rest and antiinflammatory drugs are also very helpful, but in some refractory cases local steroid injections may be considered by your doctor.

The most important thing your doctor can do for you is to figure out why you developed hip bursitis in the first place. Tennis itself should not produce this problem unless you have muscle imbalance or an abnormal gait, such as that caused by leg-length discrepancy. Muscle imbalance can be corrected by specific strengthening exercises, and a simple shoe lift can correct an abnormal gait. With a few simple measures you should be able to avoid hip bursitis in the course of even the most demanding tennis schedule.

Tendinitis

Another cause of pain over the outside of your hip is inflammation of the iliotibial band, a long segment of fibrous tissue that connects the pelvis to the knee. Iliotibial tendinitis can be caused by overuse, an abnormal gait, or leg-length discrepancy (in which case the longer leg is affected). You should treat this problem with ice, rest, and aspirin and ask your doctor whether a shoe lift might correct a gait problem to prevent recurrences.

Snapping Hip

You don't have to be a doctor to diagnose a snapping hip. The only symptom is a loud snapping sound as you run across the court, sometimes accompanied by a clicking sensation. It does not produce pain and will not limit your mobility on the court. The noise is caused by friction of the muscles and tendons across the bony prominence. This is not a serious problem, and no treatment is necessary.

Arthritis

A much more serious hip problem is arthritis of the hip joint. Hip arthritis is not caused by playing tennis and really should not be considered a tennis injury. However, as more and more older people are discovering the fun and indeed the health benefits of tennis, people with arthritis who develop hip pain are being seen on the tennis court.

Osteoarthritis, or degenerative joint disease (DJD), is the most common form of joint disease in the United States. The likelihood of developing DJD increases as you grow older. In fact, virtually everyone lucky enough to reach age 90 will have at least a mild case of this type of arthritis. Fortunately, in most cases DJD is mild and may even be visible on x-ray films without causing any pain or limitation of activity.

In some people, however, the pain can be quite severe. Hip pain is one of the most common symptoms of DJD and is often more pronounced on one side. An x-ray examination is required to diagnose arthritis of the hip. Because the x-ray appearance is quite characteristic, additional testing is usually not needed to make the diagnosis, but in some cases your doctor may want to do blood tests to exclude other forms of arthritis such as rheumatoid arthritis or gout.

You can play tennis with arthritis of the hip if the arthritis is mild. In many cases aspirin or other antiinflammatory drugs, heat, and gentle range-of-motion exercises can eliminate the pain of arthritis. If you are free of pain, you can return to the courts, using common sense as as your guide to slowly increase the amount of tennis you play. Remember to be careful: excessive exercise can cause deterioration in an arthritic hip.

In some cases the arthritis will progress despite any form of treatment. Fortunately, this is uncommon, but when it does occur, tennis is usually out of the question. New surgical treatments can be extremely helpful in curing pain and restoring normal motion. The most dramatic of these operations is the so-called total hip replacement in which both the socket and the ball of the hip joint are replaced by artificial material. Many people feel perfectly well after total hip replacement and might be tempted to return to the tennis courts. However, heavy stress such as running and tennis can damage these artificial hips. We recommend that people with hip replacements or advanced hip arthritis avoid tennis and take up non-weight-bearing sports such as swimming instead.

This may sound ominous, but remember that serious arthritis of the hip is very uncommon in younger people, and even in older individuals mild arthritis far outnumbers the serious cases. Furthermore, tennis does not cause arthritis, even if you play daily.

Other Causes of Hip Pain

Clearly, most hip pain in tennis players is not due to arthritis at all but is caused by muscle strain, bursitis, tendinitis, and other less serious problems. In addition, it is important to remember that hip pain can be a great imposter. Many problems that do not involve the hips at all can cause referred pain to the hip. Lower back problems ranging from lumbar disc disease to sacroiliac inflammation may produce discomfort in the hip with little, if any, pain in the back. In addition, disorders of the internal organs ranging from kidney stones to inflammation of the reproductive organs, urinary tract, or intestine can sometimes masquerade as hip pain. The same is true of hernias or other groin problems and of thigh problems such as strains of the hamstring muscles. Finally, just as problems outside the hip may produce pain that is referred to the hip, so too can hip ailments disguise themselves by referring pain elsewhere. When this occurs, the pain is generally in the thigh or knee, especially in children. All in all, pain or weakness in the entire pelvic girdle region can be quite tricky. You may be able to treat mild problems by yourself, but severe pain or persistent discomfort merits expert medical attention.

The Groin

Strains

Although groin pain may be the result of referred pain from the hip or back, the groin itself can be the primary site of tennis-related injuries. The most well known is the groin pull, which is among the most painful and disabling tennis injuries and can be very slow to heal. As is the case with all muscle pulls, the actual problem is either a muscle strain caused by tearing of muscle fibers or tendinitis involving inflammation of the fibrous tissues that attach the muscles of the upper leg into the pelvic bone. The groin muscles are prone to injury precisely because they are large strong muscles, which often become tight and inflexible. These muscles can be injured by sudden starts or stops, by jumping, or by abrupt stretching motions.

Because these muscles are used in daily activities such as walking, it is difficult to rest them properly, so injuries often cause prolonged discomfort. Moreover, elastic bandages, which often help other types of muscle strains and tendinitis, are very difficult to use in the groin region. It is theoretically possible to ice down these injuries the way you would an injured elbow or knee, but in practical terms most tennis players with pulled groin muscles would much rather put up with the injury than with ice treatments.

Treatment and rehabilitation. In most cases only the slow process of time heals pulled groin muscles. If you have an acute groin pull, running will produce pain, so you will have to stay off the courts until the condition improves. You should use rest and aspirin during the acute phases of your injury and then start an active rehabilitation program, which will hasten recovery and hopefully will also prevent recurrent injuries. Gentle stretching exercises can be very helpful. One exercise is to sit with the soles of your feet together, allowing your knees to fall outward and applying gentle pressure to your knees to increase the stretch (Figure 8-1, *A*). The second exercise involves raising and internally rotating one of your legs while sitting (Figure 8-1, *B*). The third stretches the hip flexors by hyperextending your leg at the hip (Figure 8-1, *C*). Each of these exercises should be done slowly, holding each position for 10 seconds of steady stretch. They are especially valuable for people with strong thigh muscles and should be part of a regular stretching routine.

Hernias

Another cause of groin discomfort is an inguinal hernia. Although this is a good deal more common in male players, it can sometimes turn up in women. You will recognize a hernia as a bulge in the groin, which increases or pops out when you cough or strain. In many cases these are completely painless, but they can cause nagging discomfort and sometimes they can even produce severe problems if they become entrapped in the groin. If a hernia is trapped, immediate surgery is mandatory. Usually hernia surgery can be accomplished electively, at a time and place of convenience. In fact, some older individuals may even elect to postpone this type of surgery and rely on a truss. Tennis does not cause hernias, and in most cases having a hernia should not prevent you from playing. Still, we recommend elective surgical repair for most active individuals. After surgery and a modest period of recuperation you should be able to return to full activity without problems.

A related question, often asked by young male players, relates to the possible benefits of an athletic supporter. Although the athletic supporter is a universal garment in men's locker rooms from junior high school onward, there is really very little medical evidence that it is helpful. In fact, some people feel that they can cause chafing, which may predispose them to jock itch. If you feel more comfortable and secure with an athletic supporter, by all means wear one. However, there is certainly no reason to recommend the use of a supporter for most male tennis players.

The Thighs

Contusions

The thigh is basically a single bone surrounded by very heavy strong muscles. Strong muscles resist injury, but when they are damaged, they may heal slowly: Yannick Noah pulled a thigh

Figure 8-1   Stretching exercises for the groin.

muscle in the 1980 French Open but recovered so slowly that he was forced to miss Wimbleton. Perhaps the most common athletic injury to the thigh is a contusion or a bruise resulting from direct trauma. Like other contact injuries, this is not a problem that is likely to be caused by tennis itself. However, if you are a tennis player who likes to step off the court for an occasional "touch" football match, you may suffer a thigh contusion. This will not impair your tennis—if you treat it right. Because there can be substantial bleeding into these big strong muscles without any discoloration of the skin, you should never massage a bruised thigh. Instead, apply ice and pressure. The infrequency of this injury in tennis players is yet another testimonial to the health advantages of tennis, particularly in contrast to contact sports.

Hamstring Pulls

The most common thigh injury in tennis players is the hamstring pull. Gene Mayer is a case in point; this accomplished pro was forced to miss the 1980 U.S. Open because of a pulled hamstring. The hamstrings are actually a group of five large muscles behind the thigh. The hamstrings run the entire length of the thigh and can be injured in their upper, middle, or lower portions.

A hamstring pull is actually a strain or tear of the muscle fibers or an inflammation of the muscle or the tendons that attach it to bone. The most common causes of hamstring pulls are tightness, muscle imbalance, and overuse. Muscle imbalance is a particular problem in this area because the hamstrings tend to be less well developed than the large quadriceps muscles at the front of the thigh, which oppose them. In normal circumstances the quadriceps are usually 50% stronger than the hamstrings. In other words, if your quadriceps are able to lift 60 pounds, your hamstrings should be able to lift 40 pounds. However, the quadriceps can become disproportionately strong as a result of many athletic activities, including bicycling, sprinting, and running up hills. This type of imbalance can cause pulling of the hamstrings. In addition, running full tilt on the court without appropriate warm-up and stretching can lead to a strain.

Treatment. The most important element of treatment is prevention. You can test yourself to find out if your hamstrings are tight by lying on your back and trying to flex your leg at the hip so that it is upright and perpendicular to the ground at a 90-degree angle. If you can't do this, you may have a hip or back problem— or you may just have tight hamstrings. Figure 3-3 will show you some exercises to stretch tight hamstrings. These are also excellent to incorporate into your warm-up routine so that you will avoid sudden stress on a cold or tight hamstring muscle.

If, despite this, you are still subject to hamstring pulls, you should have your quadriceps and hamstring muscles strength tested. Relative hamstring weakness can be treated with specific strengthening exercises.

If you have an actual hamstring pull, apply ice to acute injuries, and avoid running on the courts until you are better. Then begin gentle stretching and rehabilitation with a slow return to normal play. As in other injuries of this type, aspirin or other antiinflammatory drugs can be helpful. We would like to reemphasize that an ounce of prevention is worth a pound of cure. With appropriate stretching and warm-up you should be able to avoid having your tennis game hamstrung by this type of injury.

9 The Lower Back

The evolutionary forces that caused humans to develop from four-legged animals to ones with an upright posture surely did not allow for tennis. Body mechanics that permit comfortable standing and walking are quite different from the mechanics necessary for the forceful rotation that accompanies a good forehand or the backward stretch required for a good serve. In fact, the combination of rotation and flexion (forward bending) or extension (backward bending) is one of the major causes of lower back pain. The wonder is not how many tennis players have back trouble, but that any of us escape it.

Normal Anatomy and Function of the Back

The normal configuration of the back is a series of gentle curves (Figure 9-1) starting at the neck (cervical spine), reversing for the upper back (thoracic spine), reversing again at the lower back (lumbar spine), and finally, reversing a last time in the short segment of the sacrum and coccyx, or tailbone. The effect of these curves is to distribute forces away from the spinal column itself to various adjacent structures. The vertebral bodies are provided with strong supporting ligaments, which bind them together tightly while still allowing mobility. In addition, the muscles of the pelvis (the hip flexors and hip extensors) work with the back muscles to provide stability. If you are in good shape, the muscles of the abdomen help form a column with the lower back muscles to support the weight of your upper body. Your weight should not be carried on your spine itself unless (as too often happens) poor posture, poor muscle tone, or injury alters the normal function of your back.

Separating each vertebral body is a disc, a gelatinous pad of thick, shock-absorbing material held in place by strong ligamentous

119

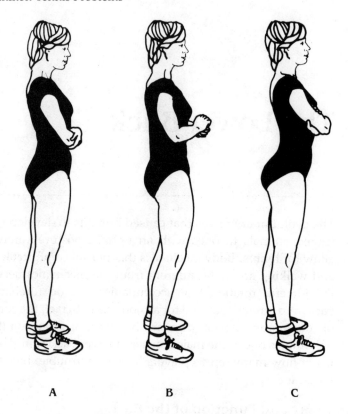

A   B   C

Figure 9-1   **A,** The normal anatomy of the back. Abnormal posture: **B,** too straight, and **C,** hyperextended posture. Note that the back is not straight but comprises a series of gentle curves. Both the straight back and hyperextended back distort these curves.

bands. The nerves responsible for movement and sensation pass along the back of the vertebral column as the spinal cord. If some of the gelatinous material from a lumbar disc is extruded, or pushed out, from its position between the vertebral bodies, it can impinge on these nerve fibers, causing pain, numbness, or weakness anywhere from the back to the toes.

Bending forward (flexion) and bending backward (extension) are the primary motions allowed in the lumbar spine. It may surprise you to learn that you have a greater degree of extension than flexion in the spine itself. Most of what passes for flexion of the spine is a combination of lumbar flexion (25 to 45 degrees) and hip and pelvic rotation. Thus a flexible and normal hip joint and pelvic girdle are important components of a healthy back. Rotation occurs primarily in the thoracic spine, or upper trunk, but some occurs in the lower back as well.

The Causes of Back Trouble in Tennis Players

Back pain in tennis players is usually produced by one of two situations: an abnormality of the back or one of its associated structures or an ill-advised maneuver that puts undue stress on a healthy back. An example of the first situation is seen in players who have tight or tired ligaments and muscles of the lower back, which do not allow good flexion. As a result, a perfectly normal stroke may cause strain, spasm, and pain. The tightness may be the result of poor flexibility, muscle fatigue from a set that went on too long, failure to warm up properly, or a drop in air temperature as the sun sets, causing muscles to cool. This tightness leads to abnormal posture and pain and spasm in the lower back and in the hamstring muscles. Frequently, pain from tight muscles may be chronic, nagging, and insidious.

Optimal fitness and good form will help protect your back, but even ideal conditioning is no guarantee against problems. Top-flight pros who have had back problems include Jimmy Connors, Marty Riessen, Dick Stockton (who wore a corset in tournaments), Martina Navratilova, Evonne Goolagong (who carried her x-ray films with her on tour), and Tracy Austin. Our exercise program should help prevent back problems, but if pain occurs, you should know what to do.

Even if your back is structurally normal, you can get back pain from abnormal or ill-advised maneuvers: for example, if you hit a low ground stroke by bending your back and not your knees, you will cause your lower back to rotate and flex at the same time. This combination forces various tissues past their normal range. The pain that results usually comes on suddenly and may be quite severe.

Distinguishing Between the Major Types of Back Pain

Musculoligamentous strain, the most common type of pain, should be distinguished from disc or nerve root pain. Muscle strain is often felt as a chronic, aching feeling across the lower back; it may be complicated by acute spasm of muscles anywhere in the back, which become tight and painful. On the other hand, a herniated lumbar or sacral disc that impinges on spinal nerve roots will cause midline back pain and tenderness, as well as pain radiating into the

Figure 9-2   Sciatica. The sciatic nerve courses out of the lower lumbar spine into the lower leg. It is somewhat exposed near the buttock and, if irritated, will be tender to the touch in this area.

buttocks or lower extremities. If the sciatic nerve is involved, the nerve itself will be tender to the touch (Figure 9-2). Sciatica, the common name for this problem, is often caused originally by a disc, but sometimes the disc itself will improve, leaving only the sensitive nerve. Finally, although disc disease and muscle strain are quite different, they often coexist; disc damage may result from repeated, smaller insults leading to a combination of weakness and muscle spasm and eventually giving rise to disc injury and nerve root pain.

Treatment

Luckily, most back pain, whether originating in the muscles, ligaments, or discs, gets better with rest. If you have significant back pain, the more you rest, the faster you'll recover. You may require full bed rest. A firm surface and even a bed board under the mattress may be in order. Lying with your knees bent, supported by a pillow, is often very helpful. Complete recovery may take 2 to 3 weeks, but in general, if the pain has not improved in a few days, a call to your doctor is indicated. Other warning signs that require prompt medical attention include weakness or clumsiness of your leg or foot, numbness or loss of feeling, or impairment of bowel or bladder function. Don't ignore these warning signs. Disc disease occasionally requires more than bed rest, and there are other, less common causes of back pain that may require a diagnostic x-ray examination, medical intervention, or even surgery.

Fortunately, most lower back pain is less serious. Besides rest and avoiding the courts until the pain is gone, some other simple measures will help. Pain medications and antiinflammatory agents such as aspirin or similar compounds (see Chapter 13) will help break the cycle of inflammation, pain, spasm, and repeated injury. Temporarily increasing abdominal support by a girdle or a lumbosacral corset can be helpful. Heat or a careful massage can be very soothing. Muscle relaxants ranging from diazepam (Valium) to methocarbamol (Robaxin) provide dramatic relief for some people. If the pain is severe, if it fails to begin improvement promptly with this program, or if you have warning symptoms of weakness, loss of sensation, or a change in bowel or bladder function, you need expert medical attention.

Rehabilitation and Prevention
Pelvic Tilts and William's Exercises

When the worst of your pain is better, begin to practice pelvic tilt exercises. Lie on your back with your knees bent, hands behind your head. Press the small of your back against the floor, and tighten your abdominal muscles. This should cause your back to flatten and eliminate the hollow between the floor and your back. It thus gently stretches the lumbosacral muscles (Figure 9-3, *A*).

The second type of stretching exercise, William's exercise, begins with the same position but with your hands by your sides. Grasp one knee with both hands, and pull as close to the chest as possible without pain or strain. Hold for 5 seconds, return to the starting position, and repeat five times, alternating with the other leg. Do not strain. These exercises are often all that is necessary to provide adequate flexibility and relief of muscle spasm to the muscles along the spine and get you on your feet again (Figure 9-3, *B*).

Back to the Court

Most players can play tennis again (1) when they are free of pain and (2) when their back and its supporting structures are in top condition. Unfortunately, most of us go back to tennis after only

Figure 9-3 **A,** Pelvic tilt, **B,** Stretching exercise (William's exercise), **C,** Cat's back exercise.

condition 1 is fulfilled, ignoring either the faulty style or the faulty body function that caused the problems in the first place. After the problem recurs a few times, prevention begins to make sense and players are willing to practice it.

Start rehabilitation off the court. Practice good posture—your mother was right! Stand with your head up, chin in, shoulders back. Respect your anatomy, and watch your weight. Sit in chairs with firm backs and seats. Use a low foot rest when sitting for long periods. Use a firm mattress. Bend and lift correctly by bending your hips and flexing your knees, keeping your back relatively straight; carry heavy objects close to your body, and get help with bulky, heavy items.

On the court, work on your style. Keep your knees flexed. Anticipate shot placement, and get into position early to avoid sudden, off-balance movements. For low shots, bend from your hips and flex your knees rather than your back. You will have less back trouble and hit better shots than if you bend and "golf" the ball. Develop smooth, fluid motions in your strokes by using your upper body to put power into your strokes and create a good follow-through.

As your style and strokes improve, work on the functional mechanics of your back with the following set of exercises designed to increase:

- Flexibility of the lumbar spine
- Abdominal muscle strength
- Lower back strength
- Hamstring flexibility
- Hip flexor flexibility
- Good lumbar-pelvic motion

Flexibility exercises of the lumbar spine. Flexibility exercises for the lower back involve primarily flexion rather than extension exercises. The first step is the so-called pelvic tilt and William's exercises, just described (Figure 9-3). They are designed to flatten out the lumbar spine, straighten the lumbar curvature, stretch the muscles along the spine, and gradually increase flexibility. They should be continued after the pain has gone. An advanced flexibility exercise (Figure 9-3, C) is the cat's back; with proper practice, it allows one to move the lumbar spine from flexion to extension.

Abdominal muscle strength. Abdominal strength is essential for a good back. As noted earlier, the curvature of the back distributes forces away from the spine. If abdominal muscle tone is good, the lower trunk acts like a column with the muscles supporting the upper trunk. If the tone is poor, posture suffers, leading to increased lumbar curvature, decreased flexibility, and an inability to carry the load. Therefore sit-ups are an important part of any back program. They should be done with knees bent (Figure 9-4). Begin with your arms by your side, and progress to the point when you can do 25 to 50 sit-ups with your hands behind your head. It is important to begin each sit-up by flattening your back (as with the

Figure 9-4 Bent-knee sit-ups. Build to where you can do 25 to 50 with your hands behind your head.

pelvic tilt). If you are so tired that you have to jerk yourself up with your hip flexors (causing your back to bow), you should stop, since at this point the sit-ups may strain your back and cause pain. Do not rush your sit-ups.

Lower back strength. Lower back strength can be enhanced by a variety of exercises, some of which are covered in Chapter 2. Begin by doing good morning exercises while sitting (Figure 9-5), first with your hands behind your head, then with weights.

Hamstring Flexibility. As noted earlier, good mechanics of bending involve pelvic rotation around the hip joint. If your hamstrings are tight, then they limit the amount your pelvis can rotate, forcing your flexion to come from your back. Furthermore, tight hamstrings pull your back abnormally straight, eliminating the benefits of the lumbar curve in carrying the weight of your upper body (Figure 9-1). Many hamstring stretches are available (see Figure 3-3). A good stretch, if you have back trouble, is to put one foot on a chair and gradually lean forward until you feel the pull on your hamstrings. Repeat for the other leg. Doing this regularly will gradually give you good flexibility in these crucial muscles.

Hip Flexor Stretching. A less commonly recognized cause of back pain is tightness of the hip flexors, the iliopsoas muscle group. They attach to the anterior lumbar spine and the anterior part of the hip and are responsible for helping create the lumbar curve. However, they frequently are tight, produce an increased curvature, and make forward flexion of the lumbar spine difficult (Figure 9-1).

Figure 9-5   Good morning exercise, sitting. With your hands behind your head bend down until you touch your thighs, then straighten up again. After you can do this 25 to 50 times, carry a small barbell behind your head. Begin with 2 to 5 pounds.

Flexibility exercises for these muscles are illustrated in Figure 9-6, *A*. Lie on your back with one leg bent and your foot as near your hip as possible. Your knee will almost certainly come off the ground because of the action of the iliopsoas muscles. Gradually stretch to the point where you can get your knee comfortably to the ground, stretching the anterior thigh and iliopsoas muscles. Hold for 20 to 30 seconds and repeat on the other side. Another good exercise requires that you get into a position as if you were starting a race from blocks and gradually lower your hip as shown (Figure 9-6, *B*). This will produce a gradual controlled stretch of the hip flexors and groin muscles. Repeat with the other leg forward.

Good lumbar-pelvic motion. Good lumbar and pelvic motion can be furthered through toe-touching, although the exercise is controversial. Done carefully, when your back is free of pain, it is the best way to regain good coordination of your back and pelvic motion. It is not necessary that you actually touch your toes.

Figure 9-6   **A,** Flexibility exercise for the hip flexors. **B,** Groin and anterior thigh stretch. Get into the lower position shown with your forward knee over your ankle. Lower your hips toward the ground to stretch your anterior thigh and iliopsoas muscles. Hold for 10 to 20 seconds. Repeat for the other side.

Rather, you should bend forward slowly, in a controlled and fluid manner to the point of resistance, hold for a few seconds, and then straighten up (Figure 9-7). This exercise should not be done if it causes pain or spasm. Also, it is important to avoid rotation while doing the exercise.

• • •

This full group of exercises, done as a set and done regularly, will remove the cause of back problems in most individuals. Of course, exercises will not correct structural abnormalities or congenital problems, which may cause pain even in the presence of good strength and flexibility. Any pain that persists or is provoked by simple exercises deserves a further medical evaluation.

Back to Tennis

When heading back to the tennis court, remember the following:
1. Warm up before hitting the ball by going through back stretching and mild calisthenics first and then taking the time to hit enough practice strokes.

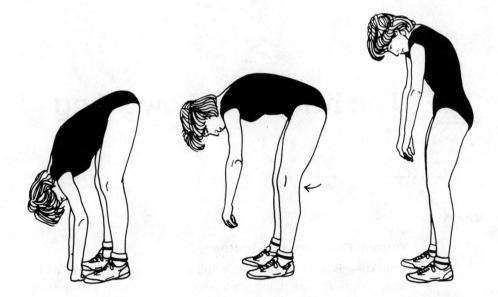

Figure 9-7   The proper sequence for toe-touching. Bend as shown, in a fluid and controlled manner, allowing your knees to flex slightly and your back to round out as you rotate from the hips. Bend to the point of tension only. Don't force yourself lower. Hang for 5 to 10 seconds, then straighten by reversing the motion, again being careful to bend your knees slightly and round your back. Repeat 5 to 10 times. As you become more flexible, you will be able to reach lower, but don't rush it.

2. Be particularly careful to practice your serves and avoid the mistake of powering your serve in if your back is giving you problems. It is the stroke most likely to send you to an early shower.

3. Protect your back by keeping warm. At the end of a long match when the air temperature begins to cool, put on a sweat suit.

4. Watch yourself carefully for a day or two following a long, hard match. Often the injuries occur then, when a minor twist may send tired, stiff muscles into spasm. This is especially true at the beginning of the season.

There you have it. Proper form, proper body mechanics, and common sense—together they will prevent back trouble in most tennis players, allow the unlucky ones to recover and play again, and help everyone to play better.

10   The Knee and Lower Leg

The Knee

Normal Function and Anatomy

The knee is a most deceptive joint. Most people think of it as simply a hinge, allowing only backward and forward motion. If that were the case, the joint would be a lot simpler, knee injuries would be rarer, and we would all be a lot less mobile.

To see what we mean, try hitting a forehand with your knees and legs straight. This locks your knees and prevents any lateral or rotary motion at the knee joint. Now bend your knee and notice how much easier it is to rotate, shift your weight, and maintain your balance—and consequently, how smoothly power is shifted from your back foot to your forward one. Your knee, when bent, allows lateral and rotational motions without which a vigorous game of tennis would be impossible.

Good tennis form is based on good anatomy. Hitting the ball with your knees slightly bent, as your pro keeps telling you, relaxes the various ligaments that hold the knee together and allows motion in a direction other than merely backward or forward. If the knee were constructed like the hip, in which the bones fit tightly into one another, this would not be the case. But the bones of the knee—the femur (thigh) and tibia (shin)—are only lined up against each other, held there by groups of very strong ligaments and muscles (primarily the quadriceps). In certain positions the ligaments are lax, allowing mobility and the kind of movement that makes tennis and other sports possible.

Knee Injuries

The trade-off for this degree of mobility is that the knee is the most frequently injured joint in sports. Luckily, knee injuries are not common in tennis, but acute injuries of the knee do occur. If you are not convinced, ask Greer Stevens. This talented pro snagged her shoe on an artificial court surface while going for a routine shot in May 1978. The result was a 5-hour knee operation, 11 weeks in a cast, and 6 months of rehabilitation before returning to play—with a 1-pound knee brace. Nor is Stevens unique—Billie Jean King has scars from three knee operations to prove this point.

Slipping on wet leaves or stepping on a tennis ball can produce the type and degree of rotary forces sufficient to tear a cartilage or ligament. Likewise, a sudden change in direction, hitting a low shot with your knees bent but off balance, or straightening suddenly as the ball takes a high bounce is the kind of motion that can cause knee injuries. Serious injuries are associated with acute pain, swelling, and stiffness, often accompanied by fluid in the joint and a sensation of instability. These symptoms should prompt an early visit to your physician, if possible, before the swelling obscures the nature of the injury and makes precise diagnosis difficult.

Ligament injuries and rehabilitation. The most common cause of acute pain is a ligament sprain. The knee ligaments are the collateral ligaments outside the knee and the cruciate ligaments inside the knee. Typically, the collateral ligaments are injured when your knee is straightened and stressed from side to side too forcibly, whereas the cruciates are injured when the knee is bent and stressed forward or backward. All the ligaments are more easily injured when rotational forces are added to these stresses.

Sprains are graded I (relatively minor stretching of the ligament), II (partial tear), or III (complete tear). All knee sprains need rest and ice to control the swelling. If it is only a minor (grade I) sprain, the principles of treatment are the same as for other injuries: frequent applications of ice during the first 2 days, elevation, elastic bandage, and rest for 3 or 4 days may be all that is necessary. When the pain and swelling have improved, you can begin partial weight bearing with crutches and gentle range-of-motion exercises. As shown in Figure 10-1, *A*, you should work until your knee can again go from full extension to full flexion. Whirlpool bath or ultrasound treatments may be helpful in hastening your knee's return to a full range of motion, but a hot tub is cheaper and more fun.

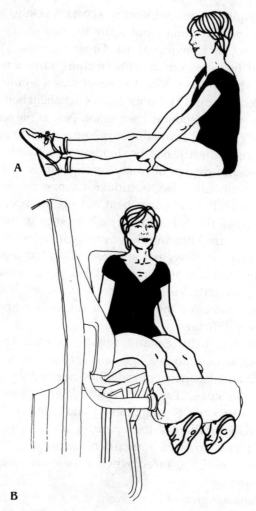

Figure 10-1 Knee exercises following injury. **A,** Isometric quadriceps sets. Sit on a floor with your legs outstretched. Link your hands under the injured knee, raising the thigh slightly off the floor. Now straighten the knee for a count of 10 if possible. Relax. Build up until you can do 10 of these. This develops good quadriceps strength with a minimum of knee motion. **B,** Knee extension exercises for quadriceps strength. These are dynamic exercises done with a weight boot weighing 2 to 5 pounds initially or, as illustrated, on leg extension machines with low resistance. These exercises should be done after the knee is pain free. Start at 6 repetitions and build up to 10 to 15 repetitions per set and 2 or 3 sets once per day. At that point you can add 2 to 3 pounds more, decrease the repetitions to 6, and build again. Continue until your knee is strong. Don't forget to exercise the other knee as well to develop balanced strength and prevent future injuries.

As the pain decreases, conditioning exercises should be started, developing good quadriceps and hamstring strength. Quadriceps exercises can range from isometrics, if there is still pain in the joint, to knee extension exercises using exercise equipment or a weight boot. The knee extension exercises should be done with relatively small amounts of weight initially (starting as low as 2 to 5 pounds), doing 10 to 15 repetitions per set, and 2 or 3 sets per day. Done for rehabilitation purposes, daily workouts are okay if you remember that slow, progressive addition of weight or resistance is the rule. Two pounds additional per week is often sufficiently fast progress. Knee stability requires strong ligaments and muscles, and your goal should be first to restore your knee strength and then to develop it as much as possible to prevent future problems. Any pain underneath the knee cap is a contraindication to lifting weight through an arc. In this situation, use isometric exercises.

A grade II sprain involves partial tearing of a ligament. The knee pain is greater and the swelling more, but the principles of treatment the same, except each stage of recovery takes longer and there may be some pain for 2 or 3 months. The knee itself is functionally stable, but restoration of strength is important.

A grade III sprain or complete rupture of a knee ligament often requires surgery; otherwise, an unstable knee will be the result. These are unusual tennis injuries. However, as those of you who watch beer commercials know, tennis players also play other sports, such as football; if you are one of those unlucky enough to have this injury, it does not mean the end of your tennis career. Rehabilitation will be slow, often lasting 12 months, but a good result can be expected. The key is to maximize your quadriceps and hamstring strength through a progressive weight-lifting program. Rehabilitation from surgery is best supervised by your doctor or physical therapist, but the principles are the same as with simpler sprains. You may also benefit from a knee brace.

Cartilage tears. Meniscal cartilage tears are another type of acute injury that can occur during tennis or from many other sports. The meniscal cartilage of the knee is a washer-shaped ring between the tibia (shin) and the femur (thighbone). It helps cushion and stabilize the knee, but it can be compressed and torn if it is caught between the tibia and femur during sudden forceful motions. Like ligament sprains, a torn cartilage can produce sudden pain, swelling, and stiffness. Unlike a sprain, a torn cartilage generally will not heal spontaneously because of its poor blood supply. Thus, even after the acute phase subsides, it may cause recurrent problems, such as locking of the knee or episodes of fluid and swelling in the knee. Many people have torn cartilages that bother them rarely, if at all, and can play tennis without problems. Often, however, the symptoms may require that the torn cartilage be removed.

Increasingly these days, both the diagnosis and removal of the torn cartilage are done using arthroscopy. The arthroscope is a small instrument the size of a thin ballpoint pen; it can be inserted into the knee joint and allows an experienced orthopedic surgeon to visualize directly the various structures of the knee. Among the things that arthroscopy has taught us is how difficult it is to make a precise diagnosis of the causes of knee pain by a physical examination alone. Another feature of the arthroscope is that, by using additional small instruments, it often allows the surgeon to remove the torn cartilage by nibbling away at it bit by bit. Arthroscopic surgery is safe and effective when performed by an orthopedic surgeon especially trained in this technique. It can allow you to be back on your feet walking in a few days, as opposed to the 2 to 3 months of rehabilitation required after conventional knee surgery.

Chronic Knee Pain

In constrast to these more acute injuries, there are many common knee problems that are associated with mild to moderate chronic pain in and above the knee.

Chondromalacia patella. Chondromalacia patella is a rather fearsome name for what is often a relatively minor problem. The knee cap, or patella, is prone to irritation and inflammation on its cartilaginous undersurface. This is especially true in women, possibly because the knee cap is often looser in its groove and is therefore subject to more irritation. The problem is often associated with forceful extension or straightening of the knee, seen, for example, in bicycling, sprinting, or jumping. The pain is usually felt deep under the knee cap and may be associated with a grinding sensation called crepitus. If you have chondromalacia, your knee will bother you most when you get out of a chair after sitting for a long time (the ''movie sign''). Usually it can be treated with antiinflammatory medication, rest, an elastic knee wrap, and quadriceps-strengthening exercises done isometrically (Figure 10-1, *A*). In severe cases you may have to see an orthopedic surgeon and perhaps avoid sports for as long as 4 to 6 weeks; even walking stairs and getting up from deep chairs can increase the irritation and should be avoided until you are better. A good stretching program for calves, hamstrings, and quadriceps is often helpful, since tight muscles are associated with development of this problem. Very rarely, chronic, severe chondromalacia may necessitate surgical repair to ensure that the patella rides correctly in its groove. More commonly, after rest, medication, and isometric exercise, the pain disappears. At that point a progressive quadriceps-strengthening program will prevent its recurrence (Figure 10-1, *B*). Again, avoid lifting weights through an arc if there is pain. Use isometrics in these situations.

Patellar tendinitis. Often mistaken for chondromalacia, patellar tendinitis shows up as pain below the knee cap in the tendon that attaches the knee cap to the tibia. Characteristically, it produces tenderness in this area so that you can reproduce the pain by pushing on the tendon itself. It is seen most frequently in basketball players and has earned the name ''jumpers knee.'' The treatment is similar to that for chondromalacia except that ice, especially after playing, is very helpful here. Rest, elastic wraps, aspirin or other antiinflammatory medication, stretching, and isometric exercises will hasten your recovery. As you improve, you can return to tennis, but continue the treatment until the pain gradually disappears. Recovery may be slow. Avoid steroid injections, however, because of the danger of causing weakening and subsequent rupture of the tendon.

Bursitis. The knee contains numerous bursal sacs that help lubricate the tendons that surround the joint. The most important of these are the bursa behind the patella, on the inner aspect of the knee below the joint where the hamstring tendons insert on the tibia, and beneath the knee, which produces the so-called Baker's cyst when inflamed. Overuse of your knee can cause irritation, inflammation, swelling, pain, and tenderness of any of these bursas. The pain of bursitis may decrease when you are playing but returns with some associated stiffness afterward. The most common site for tennis players to have bursitis is at the inside of the knee. Treatment principles are similar. You can often continue to play, but if the pain persists, rest becomes necessary. Ice, elastic support bandage, and antiinflammatory medication may be very helpful, but if pain and swelling persist, a small amount of steroid injected directly into the bursa will work wonders. Pay attention to your shoes as well; if they are badly worn in the inside or fail to support your instep, this will put strain on the inner side of your knee and can lead to bursitis at this site.

Plica. Plica is a newly described cause of knee pain. A plica is a thickening of the joint lining (synovium) that becomes inflamed with overuse, more often in runners than tennis players. Joan Benoit, for example, required arthroscopic surgery for a plica just 17 days before the 1984 Olympic marathon trials (which she won). During a careful examination of the knee the plica can be felt and twanged like a bow string, causing an exact replication of the pain. This problem may be associated with chondromalacia, fluid in the knee joint, or both. Treatment is primarily antiinflammatory medication and ice; rest will be helpful in more severe cases. If these conservative treatments don't work, cutting of the plica under arthroscopic control (discussed previously) is a minor surgical procedure that works wonders.

Loose bodies. Occasionally a fragment of the cartilage that covers the bone or a fragment of the bone itself (in a disease called osteochondritis dissecans) comes loose, causing aching pain, stiffness, and fluid in the joint. If the fragment actually breaks off, it can fall into the joint, causing the knee to lock. This problem is most often seen in teenagers and is not confined to tennis players. It is obviously a problem that requires medical attention, as does any situation in which there is recurrent fluid in the knee or in which the knee locks or suddenly gives away. On the other hand, grinding or clicking noises in the knee without any other symptoms don't require attention, embarrassing as they might be.

Arthritis. Arthritis can be caused by inflammation (such as rheumatoid arthritis), by trauma, by infection, or more commonly by degenerative changes. Degenerative joint disease, or osteo-arthritis, is a condition in which the shiny cartilage covering the end of the femur and tibia (though not the meniscal cartilage) gradually wears away. The cause of this type of arthritis is not known. There is certainly no evidence that exercise per se causes it. It is as common in older persons who have never held a racquet as in lifelong tennis players. In fact, tennis super seniors (70 years and older) are remarkably free of arthritis.

However, once the cartilage wears down, the knee joint narrows and is subject to increased wear and tear. This can lead to fluid in the joint, stiffness, thickening of the joint capsule, and formation of bony spurs. It may or may not be associated with pain.

This is a disease seen in older players or those whose knees have been badly damaged. The degree of disability and pain varies remarkably from one person to the next. Heat, aspirin, and range-of-motion exercises are beneficial, as are continued attention to quadriceps and hamstring strength. If simple measures don't help, medical attention is necessary.

The diagnosis of knee pain can be tricky. Not all joint pain is arthritis; in fact, conditions such as bursitis, ligament strain, and torn cartilage can mimic each other and may respond to specific treatment and allow you to get back to the courts. Thus, x-ray and even arthroscopic examinations are worth going through if your physician is uncertain of the diagnosis.

Unfortunately, in a few people osteoarthritis can be severe enough to reduce motion so much that tennis or even normal walking becomes impossible. Complete replacement of the knee joint with an artificial knee is possible these days. It won't get you back on the courts, but it will allow you to get to and from them, and for many people that is a major triumph.

Osgood-Schlatter disease. Whereas arthritis affects older players, Osgood-Schlatter disease affects kids—and with the increasing number of adolescents playing tennis, this condition will become more common. This is a self-correcting disorder, seen primarily in teenagers during a growth spurt, in which there is pain, swelling, and tenderness at the site of attachment of the patellar tendon just below the knee. The causes are unknown, and treatment consists of symptomatic relief with antiinflammatory medicine and avoidance of excessive activity—something that may be tough to do in these days of active tennis development programs for children.

The Lower Leg

The lower leg is probably affected more often by tennis injuries than the knee, since so much of the game depends on quick stops, starts, and changes of direction. The muscles of the leg consist of the very powerful calf, or gastrocnemius, muscle, which is responsible for propelling you forward, and the relatively small muscles in the front of the leg (or anterior compartment), which restore your foot to its normal position after each stride. Both the calf and the anterior compartment can be involved in tennis injuries.

Tennis Leg

First described in 1884, acute injuries of the calf muscles in tennis are so common that they are justifiably referred to as "tennis leg." This condition seems to be age related, predominanately affecting the middle-age player, who characteristically feels a sudden, sharp pain in the calf while serving or stretching to the side for a shot. At first, you feel like your leg was hit by a ball, but a few seconds later the pain becomes quite severe as you try to take the next step. Most likely, you will need help walking off the court because of the pain.

Originally thought to be due to the rupture of a small muscle called the plantaris below the calf, tennis leg is now believed by most experts to be due to a partial tear or strain of the inner portion of the calf muscle near where it attaches to the Achilles tendon. In fact, right after such an injury before swelling occurs, a small depression or defect can be felt in the muscle body itself.

Tennis leg qualifies as a type of overuse injury. Many players can recall an aching in their calf a few days before the injury, but they ignored this warning and continued to play hard. Tennis leg tends to occur early in the season as people start back with a rush and overwork these muscles, which become fatigued and tight. Add that to the natural decrease in flexibility that accompanies the passing years, and you've set the stage for the injury.

Tennis leg itself usually is precipitated when the knee is relatively straight (extended) and the ankle is flexed forward, thus putting maximal stretch on the calf muscle. The situations that typically produce trouble are the services or leaning forward and to the side for a ball almost out of range.

The consequences are dramatic, as we've described, and the injured player faces an uncomfortable few days. The best pain reliever in this situation is ice, applied as soon as possible for 20 minutes and used liberally for the next 2 or 3 days. Swelling may occur at the injured site and around the inner ankle and can be controlled by elevation of the leg. If there is bleeding, a dark black and blue mark may also form around the ankle a few days later as the blood finds its way down.

Walking can be attempted after the first 24 to 48 hours but may be uncomfortable; if necessary, a cane or crutch may be used. If walking is painful after 48 hours, the injury should be evaluated by a physician. Walking can be helped by adding a heel lift to the shoe, taking strain off the calf.

From here on, it's a matter of rehabilitation: continue using ice for 24 to 48 hours, then shift to heat for 20 minutes, four or five times a day, and begin gentle stretching exercises to the point of discomfort but not pain. Your stretching can be done while sitting with your leg out and a towel around the bottom of the foot so that you can pull gently. Use the stretch illustrated in Figure 3-1, B, but emphasize stretching the calf, not the hamstrings.

After a few days the acute injury will subside and you can begin more active rehabilitation. You should avoid calf-strengthening exercises until the pain is almost all gone, but you should maintain the strength of the shin and the quadriceps muscles, which tend to weaken on the injured side (see Chapter 2). Active stretching continues on the calf itself, now using the more conventional stretch shown earlier (see Figure 3-1). Walking should be the only exercise, but try to consciously minimize any limping.

After 2 to 4 weeks the pain should be gone, and you should begin active strengthening for your calf. But restrain yourself—you should not play tennis until the pain is gone and good flexibility and strength have returned. A ⅜-inch felt pad in your tennis shoe will be of considerable help for a few weeks.

Ultimately, all these injuries heal, although rushing back too soon or failing to adequately rehabilitate your leg can lead to prolonged disability or injuries to other parts of the leg. Recurrence is rare, but your other calf is at risk—so avoid too much, too soon, and continue with your stretching and strengthening exercises.

Soleus Sprains

In contrast to gastrocnemius injuries, which occur when your leg is straight, injuries to the smaller soleus muscle (which lies underneath the gastrocnemius) occur when your knee is bent, for example, while sliding on clay surfaces. This is because the soleus attaches below the knee and is responsible for controlling the Achilles tendon when the knee is bent and the larger gastrocnemius muscles are relaxed. The pain is felt to the outside under the gastrocnemius. Treatment is the same as for other muscle injuries: rest, ice, compression, antiinflammatory agents, gentle stretching, and strengthening exercises. Use the wall stretch (see Figure 3-1) with the knee bent to strengthen the soleus muscle. Strengthen the muscle by doing heel lifts (see Figure 2-1).

Shin Splints

Shin splints present many problems; there are multiple causes

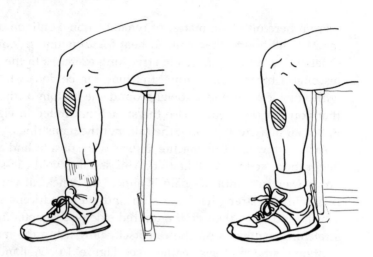

Figure 10-2   The pain of shin splints can be felt under the shaded areas on either the inside or outside of the shin.

and modes of treatment. One of the problems, seemingly an academic one if you suffer from pain in your shins, is that of definition: which of the many kinds of shin pain are true shin splints? We will not try to resolve the debate here; suffice it to say that pain in the shin area seems to be an increasing complaint among tennis players. Shin pain can occur on either side of the shin bone—the inner (medial) side or the outer (lateral) side. It occurs more often laterally than medially, and the muscles over the shin or the bone itself may be tender (Figure 10-2).

Causes. A number of causes can be defined, any of which may be important in a given player.

Overuse. Serious players spend more and more time on tennis and associated activities; the resultant musculotendinous fatigue and stress have been correlated with the development of shin pain. In players who are doing a lot of running to get into shape for tennis, development of pain along the inner aspect of the shin is fairly common.

Muscle imbalance. Muscle imbalance occurs more often in women, especially those who are new to athletics. It is easy to see how an imbalance in strength can develop between the smaller muscles of the anterior side of the shin and the large calf muscles. They are physiologic antagonists, responsible for controlling foot motion in opposite directions. The differences in the size of the muscles is a function of their tasks: the anterior muscles have only to return the foot to neutral position against gravity, whereas the calf muscles must propel the weight of the body during each stride. However, the anterior muscles must also slow the downward and backward thrust of the foot propelled by the calf. If the anterior muscles are relatively weak and fatigue quickly, muscular inflammation and pain can occur. In addition, the attachment of the muscle to the tibia or shin bone may become inflamed, giving rise to periostitis, or pain and inflammation of the sheath covering the bone itself.

Poor flexibility. Flexibility is also required for the proper synchronous function of these two muscle groups. If the heel cord and calf muscles are tight—either from overuse, the failure to do proper stretching, or the wearing of high heels—the work of the anterior muscles is increased. This again sets the stage for muscle overuse, imbalance, fatigue, and shin splints.

Poorly designed shoes. Although progress has been made in athletic shoe construction, more attention is still being paid to style and endorsements than proper function. Many tennis shoes are very rigid in the forefoot, preventing the proper flexion of the shoe at the ball of the foot. This forces players onto their toes when sprinting and puts more strain on the calves. Other consequences may include Achilles tendinitis and foot and ankle problems. Shin splints may result from disproportionate use of the calf muscle and secondary fatigue of the anterior shin muscles.

Treatment and prevention. What can you do to prevent or treat shin splints? Since the cause is multifactorial, your approach must be to address each factor. First, build up your program gradually. Don't try to recover from a winter's layoff in a week of enthusiasm. Keep a log of your activities, and resist the temptation to double your effort every day. Second, pay attention to your flexibility, especially if you have been wearing high-heel shoes or have tight calves. Do the stretches illustrated in Chapter 3 for your heel cords. You should also stretch your anterior shin and hamstring muscles. If you have developed shin splints, ice is very helpful in reducing swelling and pain. Check your shoes for flexibility at the midfoot. Do gentle strengthening exercises if your problem is associated with muscle imbalance or weakness of the anterior shin muscles. Antiinflammatory medication will help. Finally, allow some time to pass before you begin to increase your game time. Shin pain may last from days to weeks, but the conditions that led to it may take even more time to correct.

If your pain persists, it could be that you have a stress fracture of your tibia, which will require an x-ray examination or bone scan for diagnosis. Treatment is generally the same as for shin splints, but it necessitates a much longer period away from tennis. Some orthopedists apply casts, but most do not.

Cramps

Muscle cramps are as aggravating as they are common. They can occur during a match or afterward, even waking you up from sleep. They are most frequent in the calf and hamstring muscles but can occur in any muscle, including the hand or foot. Cramps are localized spasmodic contractions of muscle, which can be very painful. Some people are clearly more susceptible to them than others, but anyone can get them. The conditions associated with cramps are acute muscle fatigue from a long, hard match, dehydration, mineral depletion, falling temperature during a late afternoon game, minor injuries to muscles, or a blow by an errant tennis ball.

The muscle that is cramping should be stretched out to break the spasm, and forceful contractions of the muscle should be avoided. If you are especially susceptible to recurrent cramps, quinine may be helpful in preventing them. Small amounts of quinine are in tonic-type mixes or quinine water, but a prescription for quinine will give you a more adequate dose and better results.

• • •

As this litany of problems indicates, tennis players, like baseball pitchers, depend on their knees and legs to keep their arm in motion. Take care of them by good stretching and conditioning exercises, and they will take care of you.

11   The Ankle and Foot

Although beginning tennis players may have their first few lessons devoted exclusively to footwork, intermediate and advanced players who have mastered foot positioning rarely give any thought to their ankles and feet. Indeed, your footwork should be so automatic that it requires little, if any, thought. However, you'll start to think about your ankle or foot if you have an injury, since these problems can be just as disabling to the tennis player as elbow or shoulder ailments. Obviously your game will be best served if you can prevent ankle and foot problems before they occur. To this end, let's turn our attention to the athlete's foot.

The Ankle

Ankle problems are relatively common in tennis players. Despite their frequency, these injuries are often misunderstood and hence mistreated. The player who turns his ankle during a game is likely to dismiss the injury as "just a sprain" and to neglect proper treatment. Unfortunately, the result can be ankle weakness and a propensity toward recurrent sprains. The popular misconception "once sprained, always sprained" may cause the player to accept the problem as inevitable and fail to get proper treatment.

Perhaps you will gain greater respect for your ankle joint if you understand its structure and function. The ankle is a hinge joint that allows forward and backward motion. The ligaments at the front and back of the ankle are relatively thin to allow flexibility in this plane of motion. In contrast, the ligaments at the inside and outside of the ankle are strong and thick to provide support. The ligaments on the inside of the ankle are particularly strong and rarely sprained. They extend downward to the sole of the foot, where they provide support for the arch as well.

Sprains

Although ankle sprains can sometimes be caused by excessive forward or backward motion, it is much more common for sprains to result from excessive lateral motion. A single sudden excessive turning inward or outward of the ankle can cause an *overstress* injury or an *acute sprain*. On the other hand, repetitive overuse can cause a *chronic sprain*, which is generally milder but can still be troublesome. Both types of sprains are more common on the outer side of the ankle.

Ankle sprains may be mild or serious. In medical terms, the severity of the injury can be graded as a first-, second-, or third-degree sprain. In a *first-degree sprain* the ligaments of your ankle are stretched, but few if any fibers are actually torn. As a result, there is no loss of function and your ankle remains strong. You will have some pain in your ankle but will retain good motion. A *second-degree sprain* is more serious because the ligament is partially torn so that there is some loss of strength. However, enough fibers remain intact to provide stability of the ankle. A second-degree sprain is quite a dramatic injury. It usually occurs as a result of a sharp twist of the ankle, which produces sudden severe pain. Within minutes the ankle starts to swell and can become quite puffy and very tender. Bleeding into the soft tissues can also cause some purplish discoloration around the ankle.

Third-degree ankle sprains are serious injuries because they involve complete rupture of one or more ligaments. Both strength and stability are lost, and the ankle is swollen, discolored, and painful. You should suspect a third-degree sprain if the injury causes you to fall or is accompanied by severe pain, immediate swelling, or a tearing or popping sensation. If you have one or more of these symptoms, you should apply ice and compression bandage and head for your doctor at once. A third-degree sprain will call for at least a cast and maybe surgical repair. Prompt expert attention is necessary to prevent chronic instability, which may require more extensive reconstructive surgery in the future.

Treatment. The treatment of ankle sprains depends on their severity. You can treat mild sprains adequately yourself, but more serious injuries require medical attention. In either case, the principles of treatment are encoded in the acronym PRICE: Protection, Rest, Ice, Compression, and Elevation.

Protection and rest are important to prevent further damage and to allow the sprain to heal. You don't have to retire from your game every time you suffer a minor ankle turn. However, if you have an actual sprain with stretching of the ligaments and painful swelling of the ankle, you should stop playing before further damage occurs. In many cases, the full extent of the injury won't be apparent until an hour or two after the game. As soon as you suspect a significant sprain, get off your feet and keep your ankle elevated. The gentle application of a pressure bandage may also help, and ice is extremely important to reduce swelling. You should apply ice packs repeatedly over the first 24 to 48 hours after the injury. Hopefully, the swelling will begin to go down after 1 or 2 days, and at this point further application of ice is not likely to help. In fact, when you begin the rehabilitation phase and start to exercise your ankle, warm packs will be more appropriate.

Try to keep your ankle elevated as much as possible until all the swelling is gone. At that point you can begin gentle weight bearing, wearing an elastic bandage for support. This does not mean that you can jump out of bed and onto the tennis court. Premature return to strenuous activity is the most important cause of recurrent and chronic ankle sprain. To avoid this, you must exercise patience and restraint as you proceed through a rehabilitation program.

Rehabilitation. The first phase of rehabilitation is to restore your range of motion and flexibility. You can do this by gently moving your ankle through its range of motion. If your ankle is stiff at first, you should perform range-of-motion exercises in a basin of warm water. After your mobility is restored, begin working to rebuild strength with *isometric* exercises, done by pushing your foot from side to side against a chair leg while seated comfortably. Next, begin to work with weights, either by wearing a light weight boot or by simply filling a sock with sand so that it weighs 1 to 3 pounds. Drape the sock over your foot, and move your ankle in all directions. You may want to try tracing the letters of the alphabet with your outstretched foot. Increase the number of daily repetitions as you get stronger. When you are comfortable with this, you can start swimming or walking and even running in the pool; your body weighs only one tenth as much in the water, so this is an ideal way to begin weight bearing.

As your ankle strength returns, you can resume normal walking. When you are walking normally without any pain whatsoever, you can begin hopping. First land on both feet, and later begin a daily hopping exercise on the injured foot alone. Another good exercise is heel-raising (see Figure 2-1). The final step is running. First, jog slowly in a straight direction, and then begin to run in large circles. Even when your ankle is "normal," running can help increase its strength further. Many coaches recommend running in figure-of-8 patterns to improve the strength of both ankles.

The use of tape or an Ace bandage for support of the injured ankle is controversial because it is a double-edged sword: external support does provide stability, but it may delay rebuilding the strength of your own ligaments and prevent you from developing good flexibility. Tape can be very useful as a temporary aid; John McEnroe and Hank Pfister are among the tennis notables who have benefited from ankle taping. You should use tape or an Ace bandage to promote *earlier mobilization* following a significant sprain. Although ankle wrapping will give you stability and security, there is no substitute for a rehabilitation program. You should work to rebuild your ankle strength so that eventually taping will be unnecessary.

The painstaking process of rehabilitation may take weeks or even months, but eventually your ankle can be as good as new. No doubt you will have gained new respect for the injury that you used to shrug off as "just a sprain." In fact, you will probably want to perform exercises for strengthening your other ankle as well.

First-degree sprains can be nagging and inconvenient, but if your ligaments are actually torn in a second- or third-degree sprain, you will need a much longer period of immobilization. Your physician will have to perform an x-ray examination to be sure there is no fracture or dislocation. A cast is often required to provide strict immobilization for weeks before the rehabilitation process can begin. In third-degree sprains early surgery may be needed to mend the ruptured ligaments.

Achilles Tendon

Although not part of the ankle joint itself, a very important component of the ankle apparatus in the Achilles tendon. Whereas most medical names are obscure and confusing, the Achilles tendon is actually quite well named. Achilles was the great Greek warrior of mythology who was noted both for his strength and for the vulnerability of his heel. Indeed, the Achilles tendon shares these attributes of strength and vulnerability.

Tendons are fibrous bands that anchor muscle to bone. The Achilles tendon attaches the strong calf muscles to the heel (calcaneal) bone. The Achilles tendon transmits tremendous force every time your calf muscles contract to raise your body on the forward part of your foot. For tennis you have to spend a good proportion of each game up on the balls of your feet. The Achilles is the largest and one of the strongest tendons in the body, yet it is still subject to injuries. It is unique among tendons in that it lacks a protective sheath. In addition, it is subject to recurrent stress every time you run or even walk stairs. Finally, the calf muscles themselves can become overly strong or tight, thus increasing the stress on the tendon.

Strains and Inflammation

Whereas stretching or tearing injuries to ligaments are classified as *sprains*, stretches or tears of muscles or tendons are called *strains*. Like other tendons, the Achilles can be strained by acute or chronic overuse. These injuries are accompanied by inflammation of the tendon, or tendinitis.

You will recognize Achilles strains as a pain in your heel cord, or Achilles tendon, when you stand on your toes, walk stairs, or run. Tendinitis will produce a similar pain, but there is also an element of stiffness, which can be severe at times. Both the pain and stiffness of tendinitis tend to diminish with use, so you may actually feel less discomfort after several games of tennis. However, after you stop playing, the stiffness and pain return and may be worse than ever. In chronic Achilles tendinitis you may actually hear or feel a grating sensation (*crepitus*) as the tendon moves back and forth; nodules can form on the tendon in advanced cases, and if the inflammation is acute, you may be able to feel warmth and see redness over the skin.

Treatment. It's very important to treat Achilles tendinitis promptly. If the pain and stiffness aren't enough to motivate you, remember that chronic or recurrent tendinitis can weaken a tendon and lead to actual rupture.

In mild cases of tendinitis you may still be able to play tennis, but you should limit stress on the tendon, possibly by restricting yourself to doubles. Application of ice after you play is extremely helpful. Of equal importance are proper warm-ups. All players should perform Achilles stretching exercises as part of their warm-up routine, but this is particularly important if you have had tendinitis. Figure 3-1 illustrates proper Achilles stretches. When Achilles tendinitis is acute or severe, rest is important and you should stay off the courts and try to avoid stairs or long walks.

Another aspect of treatment is the use of antiinflammatory medications. We usually start with aspirin. In mild cases you may be able to get by with two tablets an hour or so before you play. With more severe tendinitis you should take two aspirin tablets every 4 to 6 hours until the inflammation has subsided. Many other antiinflammatory drugs can also be helpful (see Chapter 13).

Achilles tendinitis can be successfully dealt with by careful stretching and warm-ups before you play, ice after you play, and antiinflammatory medications when necessary. Two other aspects of treatment should be mentioned. *Don't* have steroid injections into your Achilles tendon. Cortisone shots into tendons can be extremely harmful because they produce weakening and thinning of the tendons, which can lead to rupture. *Do* pay attention to your tennis shoes. If you have recurrent or chronic tendinitis, you may benefit from a heel lift, at least until stretching exercises have improved the flexibility of your calf muscles and Achilles tendon.

Tendon Rupture

Fortunately, rupture of the Achilles tendon is much less common than tendinitis. Achilles rupture may be partial or complete, in which case even walking is impossible. Although Achilles rupture can sometimes occur suddenly with only mild activity, it is more common during strenuous exercise when the calf muscles contract vigorously. Achilles rupture is also more common in a tendon that has been weakened by previous inflammation. If you develop sudden, sharp, severe Achilles pain and an inability to support yourself on your foot or toes, get medical attention without delay.

Although partial rupture can be treated conservatively by application of a cast in the toe-down position, most authorities recommend surgical repair of complete ruptures. Surgery, if required, should be performed early, before the tendon becomes frayed and further damaged. If surgery is delayed, the doctor will be faced with a task not unlike sewing wet mop ends together. This will be neither easy for him nor pleasant for you—so don't procrastinate if you rupture your Achilles tendon. Although surgery, casting, and rehabilitation are a long, slow process, the results are generally excellent and you can expect to return to active tennis.

Prevention

Paradoxically, Achilles strain, tendinitis, and even rupture tend to occur in better tennis players because they spend lots of time up on their toes and do lots of sprinting on the court. They have strong calf muscles, which helps in tennis but also puts extra stress on the Achilles tendon. Tournament-level players can help prevent Achilles problems by doing exercises to maintain calf muscle flexibility and to strengthen the muscles of the anterior compartment, or shin. These exercises are discussed in Chapters 2, 3, and 10.

The Foot

Foot injuries are also quite common in avid tennis players, since each time you charge the net or retreat for a lob, you land with tremendous force, much of which is absorbed by your feet. To make matters worse, tennis involves a lot more than running. In the course of a match you will start, stop, accelerate, twist, and turn innumerable times, and each of these motions will put stress on your feet. As indoor play increases and clay courts outdoors give way to harder materials, your feet are subjected to all this pounding against hard, unforgiving surfaces.

In most cases your feet will be equal to the task. The humble foot is really a complex and intricate structure composed of 28 bones, which meet at many joints and are held together by numerous small ligaments. Whereas the ankle functions as a simple hinge joint, the joints at the junction of the rear and middle thirds of the foot are universal joints, which allow up and down, lateral, and rotary motion. In addition, the arch of the midfoot provides a springy elastic structure to absorb shock. Even the skin of the sole is well adapted to its specialized function: the skin is thick and bound tightly to an underlying fat pad, which provides additional cushioning.

Despite all this wonderful engineering, foot problems can develop as a result of the pummeling received during tennis. In fact, a whole discipline of sports podiatry has grown up to deal with these problems. Sports podiatry has taught us that subtle foot problems can actually cause pain in other areas of tennis players' bodies, including shins, knees, hips, and even the lower back and pelvis.

The Heel

Bruises. It's been said that time wounds all heels: if you play tennis often enough and long enough, you are quite likely to develop heel pain. Most commonly that pain results from nothing more than a contusion or bruise of the heel pad. A day or two off the courts should be all that you need to get relief, but if problems recur, switch to tennis shoes with extra padding in the heel or add a thin foam pad to your present shoes.

Tennis heel. Tennis heel is a minor variation on the same theme. This condition is often painless but can still cause worry because it produces purplish discoloration of the heel. If you look closely, you will see small pinpoint hemorrhages from trauma to small blood vessels, or capillaries. This variety of tennis heel doesn't require any treatment, although if you wish to eliminate the discoloration, a foam pad should do the trick.

Plantar fasciitis and heel spurs. At times heel pain can be more severe and more persistent than in tennis heel. The most common cause of severe heel pain is an inflammation of the fibrous tissues under the heel bone itself, a condition known as *plantar fasciitis*. In some cases x-ray films may reveal a second problem, the so-called heel spur. This is a region of calcium deposition and extra bone formation that extends down from the heel bone and quite literally looks like a spur on x-ray films.

Fortunately, even if you have a spur, you do not need surgery to get relief. Heel spurs themselves are not painful, but they do cause inflammation in the heel pad. For both plantar fasciitis and heel spurs the goal is to reduce inflammation. The key to treatment is a sponge rubber heel pad, which raises the heel by ¼ inch. Not only will this provide cushioning, but it will also relieve some of the pressure on the heel structure by transferring your weight forward. If this doesn't work and a spur is present, it may be necessary to get a heel cup or to have your shoes modified.

In addition to heel padding and rest, antiinflammatory drugs such as aspirin may help. Be patient and don't give up hope. With time these problems almost always resolve completely, and you should be able to play normally without pain. In unusually protracted cases, injections of steroids or procaine (Novocain) into the heel pad may be needed, but most players will recover nicely with only a foam pad, aspirin, and patience.

Bursitis. A less common cause of heel pain is bursitis. We generally think of bursitis as involving the shoulder, elbow, or knee, but in fact there are bursal sacs around most joints. The heel is no exception, and the small bursa over the Achilles tendon at the rear of the heel can become painfully inflamed. This almost always results from poorly fitting shoes and responds best to a quick trip to the shoe store.

The Midfoot

Pain further forward in the foot can be hard to diagnose precisely because of the many small muscles that can be strained and the small ligaments that can be sprained when you land hard on the tennis court. The key to many midfoot problems is to find tennis shoes with adequate cushioning and arch supports. If you have fallen arches or flat feet and are subject to foot pain, consider wearing shoe inserts. This would be best accomplished by a visit to a sports podiatrist, who can measure you for a custom-tailored orthotic device (foot support). Depending on your problem, the orthotic device can be designed to provide support or cushioning or to prevent excessive pronation (turning) of your foot.

Orthotics. The simplest and least expensive orthotic supports are made of soft material such as felt. For additional shock absorption, Sorbothane or Spenco can be incorporated. Soft orthotic supports are generally best for temporary use, especially for cushioning and relief of pain. For long-term use your podiatrist can make a cast of your foot, which is then used to custom mold a semiflexible support made of rubbery material. Semiflexible orthotic devices are ideal when you need good control of your foot motion to correct an abnormal gait. Rigid devices are also available, but these are usually not tolerated well by tennis players.

Stress fractures. Pain in the middle region of the foot often originates from the metatarsal bones. Persistent, sharply localized pain may be caused by a "march fracture," more commonly known as a stress fracture. Stress fractures are hairline cracks and tend to occur in the second or third metatarsal bone (the long bones in your foot between the toes and the heel apparatus). You do not need a severe blow to cause this type of fracture. In fact, prolonged walking or running is more often responsible for a stress fracture than is major trauma. So don't dismiss the possibility of a fracture just because you haven't been hit by a sledge hammer; a five-set match can also do the job. Moreover, stress fractures can occur elsewhere in the body such as in the lower part of your legs or even your hip.

Although stress fractures can be painful, they are not really serious. They are tiny cracks, and the bone itself does not separate. Because of this, stress fractures can be hard to detect even with an x-ray examination, and a bone scan may be necessary to make the diagnosis, particularly early on.

You do not need a cast to treat a stress fracture, which will always heal with time. You should try to stay off your foot while it is painful, but once the pain lets up, you can resume activity and even play tennis on your "broken foot." Your foot will tell you when it's safe—when the pain is gone, it's fine to play again.

Bursitis and neuromas. Another frequent type of foot pain is caused by excessive pressure on the heads of the metatarsal bones, which form the ball of your foot. Many podiatrists believe that this problem is more common in individuals with Morton's foot, a variant of normal anatomy in which the second toe is longer than the first. This results in increased stress of the second metatarsal bone, which is often evidenced by a callus under the ball of the foot near the second toe. Even for those without Morton's foot, tennis can produce excessive stress on the metatarsal heads, and this stress may cause inflammation and pain.

A metatarsal pad is the usual treatment for metatarsal bursitis. Use the pad in your tennis shoes as well as your street shoes. Finally, mild antiinflammatory drugs such as aspirin may help fight the inflammation and reduce pain. Ice can be very helpful in acute metatarsal bursitis.

Morton's name is associated with another foot problem that can plague tennis players, the so-called Morton's toe, or plantar neuroma. This is most common between the third and fourth metatarsals and produces pain that can radiate from the third and fourth toes back toward the ankle. Unlike most athletic injuries, motion and weight bearing don't tend to aggravate the pain. However, pressure does increase the pain, and players with plantar neuromas are much more comfortable with their shoes off.

Plantar neuromas are caused by trauma between the metatarsal heads, which produces thickening of the plantar nerve. The goal of treatment is to reduce this trauma. Wider shoes can help, as can longitudinal arch supports. Metatarsal bars can also be useful but will probably be easier to wear in your street shoes than in your tennis shoes. If all else fails, surgical decompression of the thickened nerve will relieve the problem.

Tendinitis. Trauma can also produce peroneal tendinitis, inflammation of the fibrous tissues on the outside of your foot from the outer ankle knob forward. This is usually caused by pressure from tennis shoes that are worn down or excessively tight. Once again, your shoe salesman will probably be more helpful than your doctor or even your podiatrist. Pick a shoe that offers maximum cushioning. A thin foam wedge elevation under the outside of your foot may afford further protection to the tendon by taking pressure off it. If the problem persists, you can try icing your foot down after you play. Finally, as with other forms of tendinitis, aspirin or other antiinflammatory drugs may help relieve the inflammation and pain.

The Forefoot

Tennis toe. If you need additional reasons to shop for tennis shoes with great care, your toes provide 10 more. Tennis toe is a common ailment in tennis players that is caused by excessive pressure on the toenails caused by sudden running and stopping in shoes that are too small in the toe box. Commonly this causes bleeding beneath the toenails, or *subungual hematomas*. Don't panic if this happens to you—it's not as bad as it sounds. Although your toes will have a purplish discoloration and be quite painful, this is in fact nothing more exotic than a black-and-blue bruise under the nail. Bleeding produces swelling, and this is painful because there is not much space under the toenail.

Your doctor or podiatrist can provide immediate relief from the pain simply by boring a small hole through the nail. This is painless and can be done easily with a small needle. The pressure and hence the pain will disappear immediately, but the discoloration will fade more slowly. Although in many cases you may even lose the toenail, a new nail should grow back without problems.

The most important thing is to prevent this from happening again. Keep your toenails short and carefully trimmed. Above all be certain that your tennis shoes are long enough and have a generous toe box—it's the best way to beat the "tennis toe blues."

Ingrown toenails. Another toe problem that can keep you off the tennis courts is an ingrown toenail. This can occur in any nail but is much more common in that of the great toe. On occasion, ingrown toenails can become infected, and these so-called paronychias require soaks, antibiotics, and sometimes even surgical drainage. The best idea is to prevent ingrown toenails through well-fitting shoes and proper nail care. Keep your toenails short, and be sure to trim them straight across instead of rounding out the side margins.

Inflammation of the toe. Ingrown toenails can happen to anyone, but there is another toe problem that is unique to tennis players: painful inflammation of the outside part of the big toe. In addition to being a problem specific for tennis players, this inflammation is confined to the right big toe in right-handed players and the left big toe in left-handed players. Anyone who has served a tennis ball will readily understand why this happens. As you roll forward on your rear foot during your serve, you put a great deal of pressure on your big toe. To prevent this problem, look for shoes with a study toe bumper and a large toe box.

Fractures. Fractured toes do not result from tennis but can occur if you stub your toe off the court. You'll know if your toe is fractured because of pain and swelling. X-ray films are usually not necessary to confirm the diagnosis. You won't need a cast for a broken toe, but you will need to sharply limit weight bearing until the pain and swelling go down. It can be very helpful to tape the injured toe to its healthy neighbor for additional support.

Skin Problems ·

Skin problems are quite common in tennis players' feet. Athlete's foot is the most famous of these problems and is discussed in detail in Chapter 12. Blisters are also covered in Chapter 12.

Corns and calluses can develop in the skin of your feet, usually in areas of excess pressure over bony prominences. You can prevent these problems by selecting properly fitting shoes, but if you get calluses, you may want to apply small pads to limit further pressure and irritation. Large calluses should be treated by a podiatrist, who will carefully shave them down or use salicylic acid plasters and appropriate pads.

Plantar warts are not more common in tennis players than in nonathletes because they are caused by viruses instead of trauma. However, plantar warts can be particularly important to tennis players because they can interfere with a normal stride, thereby hurting their game. Most plantar warts should be treated by a dermatologist or podiatrist. Many forms of treatment can be employed, but the best involves the careful applications of trichloroacetic acid or liquid nitrogen. Although surgical excision is favored by some authorities, we would advise tennis players to try to avoid surgery because the scars that result can be as painful as the original wart.

Selecting a Tennis Shoe

The common denominator in treating virtually every foot ailment in tennis players is the selection of appropriate tennis shoes. Within the past 10 years tennis equipment has undergone a tremendous technologic revolution. Unfortunately, almost all the technologic advances have come in the area of tennis racquet size, shape, and composition. In contrast, research and development of tennis shoes lag sadly behind. A great variety of styles are available, but in many cases these are just the same old shoes in shiny new trimmings.

The most important thing in picking a tennis shoe is to remember that you are the one who will be wearing it. The fact that your favorite pro endorses a shoe is no guarantee that it will fit you well. Similarly, don't let styling govern your selection. We have nothing against flashy shoes, but comfort and durability are far more important than appearance.

What are the elements of a good tennis shoe? Comfort and fit come first, and these are obviously highly individual matters. Look for shoes that have good heel counters to stabilize your heel, but avoid ones that chafe the area of the Achilles tendon. Heel cushioning should also be plentiful. The ideal tennis shoe will provide firm arch support and good lateral support to prevent sprained ankles. However, the support should not be achieved at the expense of a flexible midsole, since unduly stiff soles can predispose one toward Achilles injuries. A reinforced pivot point under the ball of the foot can also be helpful. Pick tennis shoes that have a generous toe box to avoid tennis toe, and there should be a good toe bumper to absorb the stress of your serve.

In the midst of all this attention to your tennis shoes, don't forget that high-quality well-fitting street shoes are also very important. The best tennis shoe in the world won't do you much good if you develop bunions and calluses from your street shoes. In footwork, as in so many areas of tennis, what you do off the court can be just as important as what you do on the court.

12 Heat, Sun, and Skin Problems

If winter is the season for thoughts of spring and spring the season for thoughts of love, then summer is the season for thoughts of tennis. Summertime *is* tennis time. The days are long, court time is plentiful, and tournaments abound. Tennis players feel their best, play their best, and look their best in summer.

From a medical point of view, summer tennis also affords many advantages. In warm weather your muscles and joints are less stiff, so you can stretch out and limber up much more easily than in cool weather. As a result, your play tends to be smoother and you are less prone to injuries. The general increase in your physical activity level during the summer also contributes to your overall fitness, which in turn improves your endurance. The variety of court surfaces available during the summer also affords the opportunity to play on soft or slower surfaces, thus giving your legs and back a break from the pounding they receive during vigorous tennis on less forgiving indoor surfaces.

Not surprisingly, some of our best players come from Southern states, where they have the benefits of "summer" conditions year round; the Everts of Fort Lauderdale are good examples. However, hot weather also poses some special problems for tennis players, and these are particularly severe in the South. Perhaps the trickiest problem of all is "instant summer" during a December tennis vacation to Palm Springs or Hilton Head. You'll have great tennis conditions, but you'll need to be extra careful about heat and sun, since your body won't have time to gradually acclimate to the warm weather.

Tennis in Hot Weather

Although summertime is in many ways ideal for tennis, it also poses one of the few health hazards faced by the tennis player: heat. Tennis is an extremely safe sport; whereas minor injuries are common in competitive players, serious medical problems are rare. Summer heat can produce one of these rare problems.

Hot, humid weather will tire you out and can impair your third-set skills. More seriously, summer heat can cause heat exhaustion and even heat stroke. The latter is an extremely grave medical problem, which can even be life threatening. Fortunately, these critical heat-related problems can in large measure be prevented.

Elevated body temperature and *dehydration* are the two major complications of warm weather tennis, and they are closely related. All the body's metabolic processes generate heat as an end product. The amount of heat produced is truly impressive. Even at rest your basal metabolism produces enough heat so that your body temperature would rise by almost 2° F each hour if you had no way to dissipate that excess heat. During exercise the problem is even more severe because hard-working muscles generate tremendous amounts of heat. During a vigorous singles game, in fact, your muscles can generate up to 10 times more body heat than your body produces at rest.

Although your body temperature may rise by as much as a few degrees at the end of a long, hard summer tennis match, it is obvious that your system can't allow all the heat it produces to build up in the body. Fortunately, we possess very efficient mechanisms to continuously release body heat to the environment. Most of the body's excess heat is shed through the skin. When air temperature is lower than body temperature, cooling can occur by direct radiation of heat from the body to the environment. When you exercise (or when you have a fever, for that matter), your skin becomes flushed as extra blood flows through the skin to be cooled. Another means of heat transfer is by convection; even without understanding thermodynamics you can appreciate this mechanism if you remember the welcome cooling effect of a summer breeze. The third and most important type of heat loss is by the evaporation of sweat. Even in mild weather about 25% of your excess heat is dissipated by evaporation because you are sweating constantly in small imperceptible amounts. When air temperature rises, or when you have to lose heat rapidly because of exercise, the evaporation of sweat becomes the major safety valve that prevents overheating.

To shed excess heat, the body requires fluids. Fluids are important both to allow enough blood to circulate through the skin and to allow sweating. If your body becomes dehydrated, it will attempt to conserve fluid by decreasing the amount of blood flow to your skin and the amount that you sweat. Thus your body temperature could rise disastrously. The problem facing the summer tennis player is that huge volumes of fluid can be lost by sweating. When all your pores are in action, you may lose up to 1½ quarts of sweat *per hour*. To make matters worse, you are generating tremendous amounts of heat. If fluids are not replaced, the results can range from exhaustion to shock, heat stroke, and even death.

How can these tragedies be prevented? Your first job is to recognize hazardous weather conditions. Temperatures of 70° to 80° F, which are delightful for the person engaged in quiet activities, are ideal for tennis. Temperatures above this can be downright dangerous. The reason for this is obvious: as the environmental temperature approaches body temperature, it becomes impossible to shed excess body heat by radiation to the atmosphere. Humidity is another important factor, since sweat does not evaporate well when the air is saturated with water vapor. Without evaporating, sweat will not cool you, your body temperature will rise, and you will keep sweating until you become dehydrated and possibly ill.

The first commandment of hot weather tennis is to be careful. During the dog days, try to schedule your matches for early in the morning, late in the evening, or even at night; do your best to avoid direct sunlight, which adds a great deal of extra heat. Even in the wee hours, heat and humidity can be a problem, so adjust your game accordingly. Play doubles instead of singles, play two sets instead of three, and take breaks during the changeovers and between sets. Be particularly careful if you are confronted with a sudden rise in temperature. It takes several days for your body to acclimatize itself to high ambient temperatures, and exercise should be sharply curtailed until you have adjusted. Similarly, people who are not in good condition are at greater risk of heat exhaustion or heat stroke and should avoid competitive tennis in hot or humid weather; this precaution applies especially to older players.

Heat Exhaustion and Heat Stroke

Even well-conditioned tennis players who plan carefully can experience heat problems if they overextend themselves. It is important that you know the warning signs of heat exhaustion so that you can recognize them in yourself or your partner. At the earliest and most subtle stages these warning signals may be nothing more than fatigue, loss of concentration, and a decline in tennis skills. If you continue to push yourself, more serious symptoms can occur, including weakness, lightheadedness, nausea, and confusion. If these problems develop, you must forfeit the match before you forfeit your health. Stop playing and lie down in the coolest place you can find. Drink cool fluids at a steady pace. Immersion in cool water is extremely effective, so if you are strong enough to swim, head for your club's pool or a cool shower. But if confusion or collapse occurs, heat stroke is a threat and emergency medical care is mandatory. While awaiting help, first aid should include administration of cool fluids if the victim is alert and applications of ice or iced fluids to the skin.

Fluids

Avoiding intense heat and slowing your game are important precautions, but they are by no means enough. Adequate fluid replacement is of critical importance. Unfortunately, there are many misconceptions and myths about drinking fluids while playing tennis. Many players and even coaches believe that drinking before or during a game can cause bloating, slow your game, and produce belly cramps. In our experience just the reverse is true—adequate fluid replacement will give you extra energy and endurance and is above all the major way to prevent serious heat-related problems. Your body can absorb fluids from your stomach with amazing rapidity so you will not develop bloating. Finally, adequate fluid replacement will actually help prevent leg cramps, which are often caused by dehydration.

Fluid shifts begin very early in exercise, so we recommend that you start drinking even before you start playing. In addition, your sensation of thirst will lag behind your body's need for fluids, so you can't rely on thirst as a guide for fluid replacement. Instead, you should plan to drink fluids at regular intervals even before you feel thirsty. We recommend 6 to 8 ounces of fluids during your warm-ups. In very hot or humid weather, drink another 4 to 6 ounces during changeovers and between sets. And don't forget to "camel-up" after your match is over; even after playing you may not feel thirsty, but a long cool drink will greatly reduce your fatigue after tennis.

The total amount you should drink depends on just how much you sweat. You can gauge this roughly by how wet your clothing is. If you wish to be more precise, you can weigh yourself before and after playing—but remember to remove your heavy sweat-saturated clothing to get an accurate reading. With experience you won't have to weigh in before and after each match, but it can be extremely instructive for you to do this several times early in the summer. For each pound you lose, your body is missing approximately 1 pint of fluid. A summer's singles match can easily produce a deficit of 1 to 2 *quarts*. Clearly you will need to do some serious drinking to bring yourself back into fluid balance.

What fluids are best for you? Well-conditioned athletes lose relatively little *salt* in sweat, and their blood sodium (salt) concentration actually rises during vigorous exercise. So you should actually take low-salt beverages before, during, and after your game. Supplementary salt, such as salt tablets, is virtually never necessary; a high-sodium diet can actually be harmful by contributing to hypertension. Another important blood chemical is *potassium*. Potassium is stored within the body cells, including muscle cells. With vigorous exercise, potassium tends to leave the cells, so blood concentrations may also rise. Again, supplementary potassium is not required during tennis. Finally, although a carbohydrate-rich diet provides the energy you need for long tennis matches, sugar itself delays the absorption of fluids from your stomach. Thus, sweet drinks may cause bloating during tennis.

The ideal replacement fluid has been perfected—water. Some players and coaches prefer commercial salt-sugar solutions such as Gatorade or ERG, whereas others recommend soft drinks. You can experiment and find what is best for you. It is advisable to do your testing during practice sessions so that you will have a tried-and-true game plan for fluid replacement when the time comes for that important summer tournament.

Clothing for Summer Play

In the summer your clothing should be loose fitting, brief, porous, and absorbent; lightweight cotton fabrics are ideal. Summer is a good time to return to traditional tennis whites, since light colors reflect sun and heat most efficiently. A headband will prevent sweat from running into your eyes, and wristbands will help keep your hands dry so that you will have a good grip and avoid hand blisters. In very hot weather you may even want to duck into the clubhouse for a quick change of clothing if your garb has become saturated with sweat. If you can't avoid playing during sunny, midday hours, a visor may protect your eyes from glare and your face from sunlight. We prefer visors to hats because hats prevent the loss of heat from your head and can therefore contribute to overheating. Finally, if the sun and glare bother your eyes, sunglasses may improve your game and prevent headaches. However, you should always wear high-quality safety lenses to protect you from serious eye injuries.

Summer Skin Problems
Summertime, and the Burning Is Easy

Part of that healthy ''tennis look'' is a nice, deep suntan, but the well-tanned look is not a sign of health, unfortunately. Although our culture equates a suntan with health, sunlight is actually harmful to your skin. We certainly don't want to discourage you from playing tennis in the summer, but we would like to point out the hazards of sun exposure so that you can decide for yourself, give you a few tips for protecting your skin against these harmful effects, and outline the proper treatment of sunburn.

All fair-skinned people experience some degree of sun damage at one time or another. The damaging element in sunlight is ultraviolet radiation. The various ways in which your skin responds to the sun reflect your body's reaction to ultraviolet injury. The mildest reaction is a suntan. This occurs when sun exposure is mild and gradual, so that the cells in your skin are not severely damaged. The cells do not suffer major injury or death, but they do produce increased amounts of a pigment called *melanin*, which is responsible for the tan.

A suntan does not hurt, and it looks great. In fact, a tan itself is not harmful. However, over a prolonged period repeated exposure to the ultraviolet rays in sunlight can permanently damage the skin. This can take the form of wrinkling and yellowing, which gives skin a prematurely aged appearance. If you build up a deep tan year after year, your skin may eventually look old and wrinkled rather than young and healthy. Of greater concern is the fact that repeated sun exposure will increase your risk of developing skin cancer. Although most types of skin cancer can be readily treated and cured, we'd certainly advise you to diminish your risk of contracting even this usually mild form of cancer by avoiding excessive ultraviolet exposure.

Sunburn. Even though some players may choose to take their chances with premature skin aging and even skin cancer in return for a "healthy" tan, nobody will volunteer for a sunburn. A sunburn is just that—a first-degree burn of your skin similar to what you might get from a mild scalding. Your skin becomes red, warm, swollen, and tender from intense exposure to ultraviolet rays, which will damage and even kill cells in your skin. The damaged cells release chemicals that in turn cause actual inflammation of the skin surface in exposed areas. The severity of the burn depends on how fair you are and how intensely you are exposed to the sun; sunburns are more severe in fair people who are heavily exposed without first building up protective pigments by gradually acquiring a tan. If the sunburn is very severe, your skin may even blister and weep, just as it would with a second-degree burn.

After 4 or 5 days sunburned skin will begin to peel. Peeling is the process by which your skin sheds old cells that have been damaged and killed by ultraviolet radiation. Fortunately, the skin has a remarkable capacity to regenerate, so healthy new skin will appear as the burn heals.

We are not trying to scare you with horror stories of aging skin, skin cancer, and the "lobster look." You do not have to confine your summertime tennis to the nocturnal hours. Instead, a few simple precautions will enable you to keep your skin healthy all summer long.

Common sense is the most important preventive measure. If you are very fair skinned and prone to burning, you will have to exercise the greatest care. Remember that the sun's rays are strongest between 10 AM and 2 PM. Cloudy days can be very deceiving because an overcast sky will still transmit the harmful ultraviolet rays—so be careful even in hazy weather. Cool or breezy days can be particularly tricky because the sun's rays can be just as strong even though your skin feels cool. Not even shade will give you complete protection, since up to half of your total ultraviolet exposure comes from scatter, or reflection of rays from the court and other surfaces. Remember, too, that high altitudes and latitudes close to the equator will expose you to the greatest amount of ultraviolet radiation; you will have to be particularly careful if summer vacations take you and your tennis racquet to the mountains or the south.

Early in the summer you should limit your sun exposure and increase your daily "dose" gradually. If you are very sensitive to sun, try to avoid playing in direct sunlight in midday. However, this is easier said than done. If you find yourself on the court in bright sunlight, you can get a little protection by bringing your own shade in the form of a sun visor or wide-brimmed hat. A long-sleeved jersey can help protect your arms, but remember that loosely woven fabrics will still transmit longer wavelength ultraviolet rays and will not provide complete protection from sunburn. In addition, if you wear long-sleeved shirts and full-length pants, you may get into trouble with another summer problem: overheating.

Prevention. Fortunately, there are now many excellent lotions that can block out the ultraviolet rays of the sun, thereby protecting your skin. The most common type of sunscreens are those that contain a chemical called paraaminobenzoic acid (PABA). PABA lotions are available in alcohol, cream, or lotion bases, often with skin moisturizers built right in. PABA sunscreens provide excellent protection but may stain light-colored clothing and can cause a mild stinging of the skin in some sensitive individuals.

A second group of sunscreens contains other chemicals as active ingredients instead of PABA, including padimate O, cinnamates, or benzophenones. These non-PABA sunscreens are also very effective and are less likely to stain fabrics or cause skin irritation. Most of the newer sunscreens belong to this group.

A final group of sunscreens are physical sunscreens such as good old-fashioned zinc oxide. Sunscreens in this group tend to be heavy creams or pastes and are therefore less desirable cosmetically.

Which sunscreen is best for you? All these products are effective, and you can choose the type you like best by simple trial and error. Within each group you can find out which product will give you the greatest protection by comparing the sun-protective factor (SPF) rating. The SPF is simply the multiple of time that an individual using the product can be exposed to sunlight without burning, compared with the same person not using the product. The higher the SPF, the greater is the degree of protection. If you are fair skinned and are being exposed to intense sunlight for the first time this season, or if you have had sun-related skin problems in the past, you should look for an SPF that is high, such as 15. On the other hand, if you have a darker complexion, or if you wish to acquire a tan, you can use a sunscreen with a lower number, say 6 or 10. Although we advise against sun tanning on medical grounds, if you choose to get a tan, you can safely avoid burning by gradually lowering the SPF of your lotion as the summer goes on so that your skin will gradually build up pigment instead of abruptly developing a burn.

Whatever lotion you choose must be applied properly to give you maximum protection. It's best to apply the lotion at least 1 hour before sun exposure. Because moisture will tend to wash off the sunscreen, reapply the lotion after you play tennis, swim, or shower.

Treatment. With these simple precautions you should be able to avoid a sunburn this summer. Still, even the most prudent player may inadvertently fall asleep in the sun and get a burn. If you have a sunburn, you must avoid further sun exposure until you are well on the way to recovery. Many ointments are sold to provide relief from the pain of a sunburn. Most of these are topical anesthetics (the so-called caines), which afford at least temporary relief. However, these chemicals may produce local allergies, so in general we recommend first trying repeated application of cold compresses, which are generally effective in reducing the pain and swelling of sunburn. If pain persists, you can use ointments containing topical anesthetics or even topical steroids. Skin moisturizers (such as Eucerin or Keri lotion) and zinc oxide will also aid healing and provide comfort.

Another way of relieving pain and inflammation is to take aspirin. In most cases these simple remedies will help you get. over your sunburn in a few days, but with severe sunburns other problems can occur. If large areas of your skin are burned, you may develop a fever and even dehydration, so you'll have to be very careful to drink plenty of fluids. Severe burns may also produce blistering and weeping, which can lead to infection. If your burn is this severe, you should seek medical attention, which will probably involve the use of antibiotic or antiseptic ointments plus sterile dressings until the integrity of the skin's surface is restored. In severe cases of sunburn your doctor may even prescribe a brief course of oral steroid medications.

Summertime is tennis time, and with a little common sense

and advance planning you should be able to play all summer long without developing problems from sun exposure. Just remember that it is every bit as important to stop at the cosmetic counter of your drugstore as it is to pick up new balls at your pro shop. Sunscreens and moisturizers will keep your skin in winning shape all summer.

Perspiration

Another way in which summer tennis affects the skin is by increasing perspiration. As we mentioned earlier, sweating is a perfectly normal response to high temperatures and to exercise. In fact, if you didn't sweat, you would rapidly overheat to dangerous levels during tennis. Nevertheless, sweating can produce cosmetic problems such as cracking and blistering of the skin in some players. You can try to combat these problems by reducing your body's need to dissipate heat; whenever possible, play when it's cool and wear loose-fitting, light-colored, light-weight fabrics. You may wish to use a deodorant as well, since commercial antiperspirants contain aluminum compounds, which are fairly effective in decreasing sweat production. Unfortunately, axillary (armpit) sweat glands are relatively resistant to aluminum compounds. The odor associated with perspiration is largely caused by bacteria that grow in warm, moist conditions, so anti-bacterial soaps may help make you socially acceptable.

You will have to try various brands to see which antiperspirant is best for you. Be aware that allergies and skin irritation may occur. Above all, remember that sweating is natural. The best advice we can give is to play hard, sweat freely, and then head for the showers.

Blisters

Blisters are another skin problem experienced by many tennis players. Because heat and moisture contribute to blisters, they tend to be most common during summer, but the major causes of blisters are excessive friction and pressure.

Among the most troublesome blisters are those which can affect your racquet hand. To prevent these, you should dry your hand between each point. If you are subject to blisters, it might be useful to experiment with different grip surfaces to find one that will absorb moisture best while still giving you a firm grip. Be certain that your grip size is correct; if the size is wrong, the racquet will twist on impact with the ball, causing friction. Exercises to strengthen your hand muscles will help you maintain a firm grip as well. Finally, if the blisters occur in the same spot, you can protect the skin by applying a Band-Aid before each match. If many areas are involved, a protective cloth may be useful; the thin gloves worn by golfers and baseball players are light and flexible enough for tennis. Hopefully, with regular play the skin on your hands will toughen up and the blister problem will disappear.

Another frequent place for blisters is your feet. The same principles of prevention apply here. First, be certain that your tennis shoes fit properly. Break in new shoes gradually, and keep your feet dry with powder and with absorbent socks. Cotton socks absorb moisture well, but they need not be thick and heavy. Also, if your feet sweat heavily you can dry them, apply powder, and put on fresh socks between sets. This approach seems far preferable to the older remedy of wearing two pairs of socks at a time. Finally, if your skin still tends to blister, we suggest that you apply a Band-Aid with a slippery plastic surface over the pressure points, which are most likely to blister. If you use Band-Aids, your skin will not toughen up, but this trade-off seems worthwhile if you are able to play without discomfort and blisters.

Blisters and chafing can also occur in other areas of the body that are subject to friction and moisture. The armpits and groin are common examples. Again, keeping dry is the best antidote. However, this is not always possible during tennis. An effective measure is the application of a thin layer of petroleum jelly in these troublesome areas before you play. This will provide good protection against friction, and it washes off easily after the match.

Despite these precautions, blisters may still occur. If you get a blister, don't unroof it—opening the blister will expose the tender skin below to friction and may lead to pain or infection. Small blisters should be left alone or covered with a thin bandage. If the blister is large and full of fluid, you will feel better if the fluid is drained. Your doctor or podiatrist can do this for you, or you can do it yourself. Gently cleanse the blister with alcohol. Then carefully insert a needle that has been sterilized in a flame. Make a few puncture holes, then remove the needle and gently squeeze out the fluid. Wash with alcohol, and cover the blister with a bandage until it has healed.

Dry Skin

A common skin problem for tennis players is dry, cracked skin. As mentioned before, sweating and moisture are actually important causes of dry skin because water removes the natural oils that provide moisture and lubrication. Removing excess perspiration with a towel during your match can help. Similarly, a wristband may help protect your hands by absorbing perspiration. Try to avoid excessive hand washing and showers. The most important remedy for dry skin is to replace the missing moisture by applying emollient lotions to prevent drying and cracking. Many effective lotions are available, but two of our favorites are Eucerin and Keri lotions. You should use these several times a day, particularly after showers or swimming.

Itching

Dryness is the leading cause of itching skin. However, if emollients do not clear up your itch, discuss other possible explanations with your doctor. Some people are allergic to antiperspirants, skin lotion, or sunscreens and may have a *contact dermatitis*. Poison ivy and other summer hazards can also cause contact dermatitis. Skin creams that contain steroids are the mainstay of treatment, but except in mild cases you should discuss the use of these medications with your doctor. *Eczema* is another cause of cracking and itching; this also responds to steroid creams or ointments but should be evaluated by your physician. Finally, *prickly heat* can cause a fine red rash and itch in summertime. The rash is caused by the blockage of sweat pores. Although this is not a serious problem, it can be a lingering nuisance, since treatment does not always work. Your best bet is to keep your skin as dry as possible by removing excess sweat; in addition, be sure to use emollients after you wash or shower.

Fungal Infections: Athlete's Foot and "Athlete's Body"

The most common of the superficial fungal infections is tinea pedis, better known the world round as athlete's foot. You don't even have to be an athlete to get athlete's foot; up to 50% of all adults may get it at one time or another. Tennis players are at particular risk because of the moisture that builds up between the toes during tennis.

Athlete's foot can be caused by a variety of different fungi, but no matter which fungus causes the problem, the results are the same. Most commonly, itching and fissuring between the toes is the first sign of athlete's foot. A scaly rash can also develop. In more advanced cases the skin can become red and inflamed and may even develop weeping sores and little blisters. Secondary bacterial infections may cause even more serious problems in macerated skin. Finally, the nails themselves can become involved.

The first rule in combating athlete's foot is to keep your feet dry. In addition, you can use antifungal medications. A number of effective drugs, including tolnaftate (Tinactin) and Desenex, are available over the counter without prescription. Your physician may prescribe medications such as miconazole nitrate (Monistat-Derm) or clotrimazole (Lotrimin). Many of these medications are available as powders, which can be used to keep your feet dry as well as to fight the fungus. It is also a good idea to use creams or ointments containing these drugs. They should be gently rubbed into the skin at least twice a day until the problem has resolved.

If your nails are heavily involved, or if you have a severe case of athlete's foot, topical treatments will not do the trick. You will have to see your doctor, who can confirm the diagnosis by scraping the fungus off and looking at it under the microscope. You may then need to take medications such as griseofulvin or ketoconazole in pill form. Unfortunately, these drugs must be taken until the old infected nail has grown out and has been replaced by new healthy nail tissue; 6 weeks or more may be necessary.

Another fungal infection that can plague tennis players is tinea cruris, better known in the locker room as "jock itch" or "ring-worm." Tinea cruris affects men more commonly than women, and because it is aggravated by moisture and friction, it is more common during the summer and in overweight players. In typical cases the upper inner thigh and groin are involved. A brownish discoloration, itching, and scaling are the most common symptoms. You may also note minute blisters at the edge of the rash. The margins themselves are sharply defined. Although this type of rash itches and is annoying, it is not really serious.

To treat or prevent jock itch, try to keep your thighs dry, especially after games and after showers. Irritation from your shorts rubbing against your skin can also aggravate the problem, so you may want to use petroleum jelly just before playing. To fight the fungus itself, use the same types of creams, lotions, and powders that are effective against athlete's foot. If your skin is very inflamed and sore, boric acid compresses or a dilute 1% solution of gentian violet can be soothing. In such severe cases you should, of course, see your doctor, who may want to prescribe griseofulvin or ketoconazole pills.

Insect Bites

Bee stings are never pleasant, but for most of us they mean little more than temporary pain and some itching. This can be helped by cold compresses, simple lotions, or, if the swelling persists, antihistamine tablets.

However, for some people bee stings can be a life-threatening problem. A dramatic example is Bobby Riggs, who had a severe allergic reaction from a bee sting during the 1979 U.S. Open. Approximately 2 million Americans are highly allergic to insect venom, and at least 40 die each year from reactions to insect stings. About half of these victims had no previous history of allergy—so you should be familiar with the early warning signs.

Bee stings almost always cause pain, swelling, and redness at the site of the sting. If you are not allergic, you should be able to complete your match without defaulting by applying an ice pack to the sting during changeovers. However, if you experience swelling, itching, or hives over your entire body, you should get medical attention as soon as possible. Weakness, fainting, wheezing, and trouble swallowing or breathing may signal the onset of anaphylaxis, or shock. These symptoms usually occur within an hour of the sting, and they require emergency medical treatment.

If you think you are allergic to insect venom, have an allergist test your skin. With careful injections of small amounts of venom or insect extracts on a regular basis, you can be desensitized and protected from courtside catastrophies. Desensitization shots should obviously be given *before* the peak insect season, which is in late summer and early fall. If you are allergic to bee stings, you should wear a Medic-Alert bracelet saying so. You should also bring an emergency bee sting kit to courtside. These kits contain adrenaline and other emergency medications. Teach your partner how to use them so that you can get help even if you are disabled. Actually, all tennis clubs and tournaments should have these kits available and should have someone who knows how to use them in an emergency.

Even if you aren't highly allergic to venom, you can take steps to avoid stings. Cover all food, and dispose of leftovers promptly (Riggs was stung on the lip while drinking from a can of soda). Don't wear bright-colored clothing or use perfumes, which may attract bees during the insect season. Insect repellants may also help. With these precautions you should be able to get the protection you need so that you can forget the bees and concentrate instead on stinging the ball.

13 Commonly Prescribed Tennis Medications

Tennis players vary tremendously in style and ability, but we all share one goal: to play vigorous tennis without injuries. You can prevent many injuries by preparing yourself properly. Exercises to promote flexibility, strength, and endurance, gradual warm-ups before and after matches, carefully chosen equipment, and appropriate time-out between matches will all help.

Even with the best preparations, however, minor injuries of muscles and tendons will still occur from time to time. Many injuries can be treated with various combinations of rest and rehabilitation, elastic bandages, and ice or warm packs. In some cases medications are also helpful. A confusing array of drugs is available, some of which you can buy over the counter and some of which require a physician's prescription. To make matters worse, many of these medications are available under both a brand name and a chemical, or generic, name. In general, generic drugs are less expensive but are just as effective and safe as their brand name equivalents. You need to know enough about these medications to be a smart and safe consumer of them.

The most important categories of drugs used for tennis injuries are antiinflammatories, analgesics, and muscle relaxants. Some medications act in one way only, whereas others have a dual purpose.

Antiinflammatory Medications

Antiinflammatory drugs are the most useful for tennis injuries. These medications work to reduce swelling and inflammation in injured tissues. As a result, they reduce discomfort and speed healing—hopefully enabling you to pursue active rehabilitation and then get back on the court.

171

Aspirin

Aspirin, the oldest antiinflammatory drug, is still the most useful for athletic injuries. For minor problems, such as mild tendinitis, as little as two tablets (600 mg) may do the trick. Some players with chronic inflammation benefit from two tablets before each match. For more severe problems higher dosages are needed, such as 2 or 3 tablets every 4 hours up to a maximum of 10 to 12 tablets per day. Remember that aspirin is not a cure-all; if you do not get relief—or if you still need regular doses after 7 to 10 days—you should consider other approaches to your problem, such as seeing a doctor.

Although aspirin is a safe medication, side effects may occur, particularly when high doses are used. The major side effect is stomach irritation, which can even lead to bleeding and ulcers. Ringing of the ears may occur. Aspirin can also interfere with blood clotting, but this does not cause problems for most people.

Aspirin is available in numerous preparations, either alone or in combination with other ingredients. As a rule, we recommend the least expensive formulation of plain aspirin. The exception to this rule is that, if you have stomach irritation, you should use a form of aspirin that protects your stomach. Bufferin and Ascriptin, which contain antacids, have been widely used for this purpose. Enteric-coated aspirin (Ecotrin) is even easier on the stomach, and we recommend trying this new form of an old drug if you cannot tolerate regular aspirin. It is also important to take your aspirin with milk, meals, or antacids rather than on an empty stomach. If you have a history of ulcers or gastritis, consult your physician for intructions.

Indomethacin and Phenylbutazone

Many other antiinflammatory drugs are available, but they require a physician's prescription. In some cases they may be more potent than aspirin, but they are more expensive and may have side effects, so they must always be used under medical supervision. Two old standbys are indomethacin (Indocin) and phenylbutazone (Butazolidin). In addition to stomach irritation, these drugs can produce fluid retention and can affect the nervous system. Phenylbutazone can also sometimes depress blood cell formation by the bone marrow, so we tend to prefer indomethacin, which should always be taken with milk or meals.

The New Family of Antiinflammatories

In the past few years a number of new antiinflammatory drugs have been introduced, and more are on the way. These medications are all members of the so-called nonsteroidal antiinflammatory drug family—in other words, they are interrelated chemicals that fight inflammation without having the side effects of cortisone and other steroid hormones. These new medications are being used principally for arthritis, but they may be beneficial for the inflammation caused by tennis injuries. All these drugs require a doctor's prescription.

The new nonsteroidal antiinflammatory drugs seem to fight inflammation in a manner similar to aspirin. And like aspirin, their major side effect is stomach irritation. Therefore, in general, we recommend trying aspirin first. If aspirin fails to do the job, discuss these newer drugs with your doctor. They may be more potent than aspirin for you, and many people note less stomach irritation. In addition, these drugs are more convenient because you will only need 1 to 4 pills per day instead of 8 to 12 aspirin tablets. That's the good news—the bad news is that they are considerably more expensive than aspirin.

Your doctor will decide with you which of these drugs you should try first and will discuss dosage and side effects, but to familiarize you with their names, we will list both the chemical, or generic, name and also the brand name (in parentheses) for each drug: ibuprofen (Motrin, Rufen), naproxen (Naprosyn, Anaprox), fenoprofen (Nalfon), tolmetin (Tolectin), sulindac (Clinoril), meclofenamate (Meclomen), and piroxican (Feldene). This is a confusing choice, to be sure, which is why physicians will have you start with the medication they know best and switch to another only if you fail to respond or have side effects and still need antiinflammatory treatment.

Cortisone

The steroid hormones such as cortisone and its derivatives are by far the strongest antiinflammatory drugs. As a result, they are the fastest way to settle down painful inflammation of tennis elbow or bursitis of your shoulder. Still, don't rush to ask your doctor for a prescription for steroid tablets, since these potent medications have many potentially serious side effects if they are taken as pills or injections for prolonged periods. Because of these side effects, systemic steroids should almost *never* be given for athletic injuries. Using systemic cortisone for a tennis injury would be something like trying to hit an ant's right knee with a sledge hammer: you might get the job done, but the side effects of this overkill approach would exceed its benefits.

Steroid hormones also can be injected directly into inflamed tissues such as joints, bursas, and tendons. These are the "cortisone shots" given to professional athletes so they can get on with an important game; although the general name cortisone is used in the newspapers, other closely related steroids (such as triamcinolone) are used more often. Such injections are very potent antiinflammatory treatments, and they can sometimes be combined with local anesthetics such as procaine (Novocain) to kill pain rapidly and effectively. The local anesthetic will wear off in a matter of hours, but the steroid will start to work soon thereafter. Since they are usually given in a slow-release microcrystalline depot form, the steroid's antiinflammatory effect may last for weeks or even months.

With all powerful medications you may pay a price for effectiveness, and local steroid injections are no exception. Although you will not get the serious problems caused by long-term oral steroid usage, steroid injections have their own potential problems. The greatest worry is thinning and weakening of tendons, which can even lead to rupture of a tendon. The skin over the injection site may thin or atrophy if the injection is too superficial. Although less common, infection is another potentially serious side effect of local steroid injections.

In most cases local injections of steroids by a trained physician are safe and particularly worthwhile when the alternative is surgery. Because of potential side effects, steroid shots should be reserved for chronic problems that have not responded to standard treatments such as the use of ice, heat, physical therapy, and nonsteroidal antiinflammatory drugs. Even when steroid injections are used, they should be used selectively and carefully. In general, we recommend no more than two or possibly three injections spaced at least a month apart. Injections directly into tendons are undesirable because of the risk of tendon rupture.

Analgesic Medications

The second major group of drugs that may be useful for tennis injuries is analgesics, or pain killers. These medications will make you more comfortable, but they will not fight inflammation or promote healing.

Acetaminophen

A mild analgesic that you can buy over the counter is acetaminophen—available as Tylenol, Datril, and many other brands. Acetaminophen causes less stomach irritation than aspirin, but it doesn't fight inflammation the way aspirin does. Aspirin is as potent against pain as acetaminophen. Unless your stomach cannot tolerate it, aspirin is preferred for tennis injuries because it is both antiinflammatory and analgesic. Many of the prescription antiinflammatory drugs discussed earlier will also reduce pain.

Potent Pain Killers and Narcotics

The stronger analgesics may be harmful by masking pain and giving you a false sense of well-being so that you may try to play again before your body is ready. They are available only by prescription and should be used only for very painful problems while you are under a doctor's care. Examples of prescription analgesics are codeine, oxycodone (Percodan, Percocet), propoxyphene (Darvon), and pentazocine (Talwin). These medications provide effective pain relief, which is obviously important if you have a serious injury. However, they all have potential side effects, and some may even be habit forming. So use them only if you need them and only under your doctor's supervision and instruction. Use as little of these medications as possible, and try to switch to a milder analgesic as soon as possible. As a rule of thumb, if your pain is strong enough to require a prescription analgesic, your body probably has not recovered from your injury enough for you to resume tennis.

Muscle Relaxants

The last group of drugs discussed here is the muscle relaxants. When muscles are injured or stretched abnormally, they often go into spasm. These spasms cause stiffness and pain and can provoke inflammation of joints and tendons. Heat, rest, and physical therapy will help fight muscle spasm. Whirlpool treatments, ultrasound, and galvanic stimulation are also advocated by many physicians to relax muscles. In difficult cases, muscle-relaxing medications are very beneficial as well.

Muscle relaxants are prescription drugs and require medical supervision. Examples are diazepam (Valium), methocarbamol (Robaxin), carisoprodol (Soma), and orphenadrine (Norflex). This type of medication is used most often to treat spasms of the strong muscles of the back or neck. They are effective and can be important aids to your recovery from a tennis injury that involves muscle spasms. Like many medications, these drugs have potential side effects, so they should be used only when needed and always under a doctor's orders. You should never use these drugs as your only form of treatment. Instead, when muscle relaxants are used, they should be part of a comprehensive program that includes antiinflammatory or analgesic drugs, heat, and rest or even traction.

Another muscle problem that plagues some tennis players is cramps. Like muscle spasms, cramps are basically muscle contractions that are excessively strong and therefore painful. Cramps tend to be relatively brief, but they make it impossible to go on with your game during the few minutes they last. Cramps can come in groups so that you feel miserable for hours.

Cramps are usually caused by overuse of muscles, fatigue, and imbalance of muscular strength. The best treatment is prevention by means of overall conditioning and exercises for strength and flexibility, as discussed in Part I. Another major cause of cramps is dehydration; not surprisingly, water is the best way to prevent this variety of cramps.

Medications play a minor role in the treatment of most cramps. Conditioning and hydration will usually prevent cramps, but if you get one anyway, the best treatment is to stop playing at once and to apply a gentle static stretch to the muscle that is cramped up. If you are subject to recurrent cramps, one medication may be worth discussing with your doctor. Quinine is an old-fashioned but very effective remedy for painful nighttime leg cramps. Although it is not generally prescribed for the prevention of cramps in athletes, we have found it to help a few players. Quinine is a safe medication, so if you are subject to recurrent cramps, it may be worth a try.

Unapproved Drugs: DMSO

Antiinflammatories, analgesics, and muscle relaxants are all well-established drugs for the treatment of tennis injuries, but like many other athletes, tennis players are so eager to return to play after an injury that they are often tempted to try self-treatment with unproved medications. Most often, self-medication takes the form of nutritional supplements such as vitamins and minerals, which are discussed in Chapter 15. Recently an altogether different drug is gaining underground popularity among some tennis players: dimethyl sulfozide, or DMSO.

DMSO was discovered by a Russian chemist in 1866. DMSO is a by-product of paper manufacturing and is widely used as an industrial solvent. Interest in medical use of DMSO began at least 20 years ago. DMSO is rapidly absorbed into the body after it is painted on the skin, and because it is a potent solvent, there has been interest in DMSO as a vehicle to carry other drugs into the body. It has also been claimed that DMSO by itself is a pain killer and antiinflammatory. Because of this, DMSO has been used for bruises, sprains, tendinitis, bursitis, and arthritis. All in all, hundreds of thousands of people have tried DMSO for these various purposes.

Can 100,000 users be wrong? The fact is that DMSO has not been proven to be helpful for any of these conditions. Unfortunately, there are just not enough scientific studies to determine definitively if DMSO has any benefit for athletic injuries. Studies of DMSO began enthusiastically in the early 1960s but came to a crashing halt in 1965 when experiments showed that DMSO can cause cataracts in animals. No eye damage has been shown to result from short-term, low-dose DMSO usage in humans. The U.S. Food and Drug Administration has allowed testing of DMSO to resume under tight controls, but there have been only a few applicants thus far.

Tennis players should be particularly interested in a 1981 study at the University of Arizona. Over 100 patients were treated with DMSO during a 1-year trial period. These patients were troubled with tennis elbow or with rotator cuff tendinitis, which is also common in tennis players. The physicians who conducted this carefully controlled study concluded that ''DMSO alone is ineffective in treating tennis elbow or rotator cuff tendinitis.'' Although other ailments were not studied, there is at present no evidence to prove that DMSO will alleviate any tennis-related problem.

In the United States the only approved human use of DMSO is a 50% solution for interstitial cystitis, a rare type of bladder inflammation. In Canada a 70% solution is approved for another rare disease called scleroderma. Ninety percent DMSO is available for veterinary use in nonbreeding dogs and horses, and a 99% solution is available to any purchaser as an industrial ''degreaser solvent.'' Unfortunately, a number of athletes, including some well-known tennis players, have turned to the unapproved use of DMSO for injuries and inflammation.

Although federal law restricts the human use of DMSO, it is openly advertised in many sports magazines and is easily available by mail order. It is unknown whether it is safe. Concentrated DMSO solutions produce redness and burning of the skin. Industrial preparations may contain potentially harmful impurities. Even purified DMSO can bring unwanted impurities into your system by dissolving cosmetics or other chemicals on your skin and carrying these substances right into your bloodstream. Because it is rapidly absorbed, it travels through the skin to your whole body, not just to your aching tendon. This is why users note a characteristic garlic taste and odor within minutes of rubbing DMSO on the skin. Eye damage results from prolonged use of DMSO in animals, but it's unknown whether it would have the same effect on humans.

DMSO is a unique and intriguing chemical. As an industrial solvent it's probably great, but for tennis injuries it's a totally unknown quantity: we don't know if it works, and we don't know if it's safe. Of course, players want to recover from injuries as quickly as possible, but we would advise avoiding DMSO until careful, objective scientific studies clarify its potential benefits and side effects.

Hazardous Drugs: Male Hormones, Amphetamines, and Street Drugs

While we are on the subject of unapproved medications, we should say a word about the use of drugs to "improve" athletic performance, and a word is all we need: don't. Unfortunately, some competitive athletes use anabolic steroids such as the male hormone testosterone to build muscle mass, narcotics or cocaine to get "up" or to mask pain, or amphetamines for "pep." All these medications can have serious side effects, and some (such as amphetamines) have even been associated with sudden death during competition. It's fine to take your tennis seriously—but not at the expense of your health.

Prescription Medications

Even for people who need daily medications for medical problems such as high blood pressure or allergies, tennis is almost always safe. Needless to say, if you require medications or have chronic medical problems, you should check with your physician and be particularly careful about any additional drugs you may take for minor tennis ailments.

• • •

Many tennis injuries can be prevented, and when problems occur, they will usually respond to simple treatment programs. On occasion, however, medications are also needed. Hopefully, this overview will help you understand the various medications available. Your goal should be to use them as little as possible as temporary aids that will enable you to return to form as quickly as possible.

14 Courtside First Aid and Clubhouse Treatment of Common Tennis Ailments

Since tennis is so popular, there may be a nurse or physician playing nearby at most active courts. However, in case you or your partner is faced with an injury, here are some simple pointers for dealing with common problems.

The Unconscious Athlete (or Spectator)

The problem of unconsciousness is rare in tennis but is all the more worrisome for that reason. Whether it is caused by choking, seizures, concussion, or heart attack, the initial response is the same: follow the ABC's—check that the *airway* and mouth are patent; make certain the victim is *breathing* (if not, support respiration artificially); and then check for *circulation* (if no pulse is present, begin cardiac massage). Learn the Heimlich manuever for choking and cardiopulmonary resuscitation. They are important for all of us to know and should be a requirement for anyone professionally involved with the public.

Sprains and Strains

The old standbys of rest, ice, and elevation to ease swelling and pain are the first steps. Often compression of the area with an elastic bandage will help. It is important to treat these injuries as soon as possible to decrease inflammation and subsequent swelling, pain, and disability. Definitive diagnosis and treatment, if the injury is severe enough, will have to await the attention of a doctor or trainer.

Insect Stings

To minimize the chances of being stung, avoid colognes and bright-colored clothes, which may attract insects. If you do get stung, the swelling and redness can be treated with ice initially, and the itching can be helped by an antihistamine available over the counter. Apart from the local discomfort, most bites should pose no problem. However, some people have a hypersensitivity, or allergic, response to stings. It is important to recognize this because it can evolve into a life-threatening situation. Allergic reactions are characterized by swelling and hives far from the actual sting. The most dangerous is swelling in or about the windpipe or throat, producing difficulty breathing or swallowing. If injectable adrenaline is available (in so-called bee sting kits), use it! Then call a rescue squad. If you had such an allergic response, even if it was mild, get a bee sting kit and keep it near you while you are outdoors. You should also consult your physician about desensitization shots.

Cramps

The cause, or more likely, causes of cramps are not fully known. Cramps are involuntary spasms in muscles. Although cramps do not damage muscles, they are extremely painful and can be disabling. Dehydration, muscle weakness, overexertion, the use of certain medicines such as diuretics, and minor trauma can all cause cramps. In most cases a cramp is best treated by gently stretching out the affected muscle. Thus a cramp in the calf is relieved by any exercise that puts tension on it and stretches it, like the wall push-ups recommended earlier. If stretching doesn't work, massaging the area and applying ice may help. Rest is important as well. If your cramps are mild and are relieved by first-aid means, you can carefully resume play. If you are prone to cramps in the heat, be especially careful to drink lots of water.

In some players with recurrent cramps a prescription of quinine tablets can help. Even as small an amount of quinine as is found in tonic water may help some individuals.

As with so many other tennis problems, the best way to treat muscle cramps is to *prevent* them through good hydration, developing endurance, doing your stretching and warm-up, and paying attention to good technique and form so that you don't suddenly overstress a muscle with an off-balance lunge.

Blisters

Blisters on hands and feet are a product of excess moisture, heat, friction, and pressure. Prevention is best: use proper equipment (shoes and racquet grips that fit); keep your skin dry with powder, towels, wristbands, cotton socks, etc.; protect your hand with a glove; and, finally, use a Band-Aid over the pressure points that get recurrent blisters until the skin toughens.

If you have a blister, don't unroof it. The skin underneath is very tender. Cover it for a few days with a Band-Aid. If it is large, your doctor can drain it antiseptically. If it has opened, treat it like a scrape—keep it clean, use an antiseptic ointment, and cover it with a bandage.

Sunburn

Prevent sunburn by using a sunscreen with a sun-protective factor (SPF) of 4 to 15, depending on how easily you burn. Sunburns range from mild, local redness (for which a few aspirin are necessary) to a true second-degree burn with blistering. If your burn is painful, extensive, or deep, get medical advice.

Eye Injuries

Unlike racquetball, where an eye can be injured from a racquet blow, or squash, where a small ball can actually hit the eye, in tennis the tennis balls tend to hit the bony orbit surrounding the eye. Still, frequently, the eye itself can be hit during a fierce volley. An ice pack plus a trip to an ophthalmologist or emergency room for a look at the retina is the course to be followed. (See Chapter 4 for details.)

Nosebleeds

Almost all simple nosebleeds, if caused by an errant ball, will stop if gentle pressure is applied for 5 to 10 minutes. If the nose is swollen or distorted, a trip to the emergency ward and an x-ray examination are necessary to rule out a fracture. Ice packs are very helpful.

Cuts and Scrapes

Cuts require local cleansing with soap and large volumes of tap water. Antiseptic agents are not necessary. Pressure and ice usually control bleeding. However, if the cut enters muscle, is more than 1 inch long, enters a joint space, or is associated with continued bleeding (as is often case with lacerations of the scalp), it deserves professional attention and possibly stitches. Remember, any cut, not just puncture wounds with rusty nails, necessitates a tetanus booster. Scrapes or abrasions should be cleansed promptly and covered with local antibiotic ointment and a sterile dressing to protect them. If the abrasion is large or becomes infected, see your doctor.

Fractures

Uncommon as fractures are in tennis, they can occur. Courtside first aid means immobilization. If necessary, tape the victim's arm or leg gently to a racquet in the position in which it is found to prevent further movement and damage. Then head for the nearest emergency ward.

Dislocations

Although infrequent, shoulder dislocations do occur on the courts. Unless you have had specific experience with reducing a dislocation, leave it to a professional. A sling can help while you are bringing the disabled player to an emergency ward.

Knee Injuries

A slip on wet surface with the knee bent or a sudden forceful motion may cause an internal derangement of your knee such as a torn cartilage or sprained ligament (Chapter 10). It will be difficult, if not impossible, to walk, and swelling can occur rapidly or within 24 hours. See an orthopedist as soon as possible, since the diagnosis is quickly obscured by swelling. For some injuries, especially torn ligaments, early operative repair may be necessary. The usual symptomatic measures (ice packs, bandages, etc.) should be temporizing measures only for any knee injury in which simple walking is painful.

Tendinitis and Bursitis

Tendinitis is inflammation of the tendinous attachment of muscle to bone, and bursitis is inflammation of the lubricating sacs (bursas) that help them move smoothly. Tendinitis hurts when you move the affected muscle; bursitis tends to ache all the time. Aspirin, ice, and elevation are the mainstays of early treatment. For specific injuries, see the relevant chapters.

Muscle Rupture

A muscle rupture is usually heralded by sudden pain and swelling in the calf, quadriceps, or upper biceps muscles during motion. Ice can be used to reduce the swelling, but surgical repair may be necessary and an early evaluation by a physician is extremely helpful. Thus these injuries also require prompt medical attention.

Heat Exhaustion and Heat Stroke

Although heat-related problems are covered in Chapter 12, they are so important that we will review the first-aid aspects here. Be alert to the effect that high temperature and humidity can have on you or your opponent. Don't assume that it's your brilliant play that is making your opponent dizzy. Lightheadedness, confusion, vomiting, headaches, and flushed skin with decreased sweating are the early signs of heat exhaustion.

Get victims out of the sun, lying flat, and cool them down by applying cold water or ice packs or even by immersing them in ice water. Drinking cold water is good, but only if the player is coherent and able to swallow. Call the rescue squad and transfer the victim to the hospital if improvement does not occur promptly—this is a true emergency but one that will have a happy ending if handled promptly and correctly.

Blows to the Genitalia

A blow to the genitalia in men or women can be painful and cause a serious injury if swelling, bleeding, or tears occur. Ice treatment, if tolerated, will reduce the swelling somewhat, but any discomfort that persists deserves evaluation by a physician.

Treatment Modes

Tennis Kit

Besides an extra racquet, sweatband, and can of balls, you should find room for the following in your tennis bag: an Ace bandage, Band-Aids, Vaseline, a tube of bacitracin (antibiotic) ointment, 1-inch wide adhesive tape, aspirin, and an extra pair of socks. If you are allergic to bees, add a bee sting kit. A good sunscreen visor or hat will protect you during the hot months.

Liniments

Liniments are compounds that cause a local skin reaction and a sensation of warmth when rubbed onto the skin. Liniments can be mildly helpful in superficial strains that respond to heat. They do not produce enough heat to affect structures lying more than a little below the skin. In general, if heat is useful, other modes of applying it are better.

Whirlpool

Whirlpools provide warmth, some mild massaging action, and, most of all, the ability to move a limb through a full range of motion without weight bearing. When used as part of a comprehensive program of rehabilitation, it can be very helpful. A hot tub is a useful alternative for the home.

Sauna

Like exercise equipment, saunas are becoming more available as tennis clubs upgrade their facilities. Saunas are probably more useful in relaxing your mind than your body, but they do seem to help reduce muscle fatigue after a long, hard match. Used cautiously, they are safe, but don't stay in for longer than 5 to 10 minues. Don't use a sauna if you are dehydrated or have a heart problem.

Wrapping and Taping

Elastic bandages are used for two reasons: (1) for compression after an injury to reduce swelling and (2) for chronic problems such as chondromalacia or tennis elbow to reduce pain and inflammation while allowing you to continue to play. They are generally wrapped around the limb above the area of pain to anchor them and then wrapped in a figure-of-8 fashion, with the bandage crossing at the site of pain or swelling where the maximum pressure is wanted. Wraps should not be so tight that they cut off circulation, cause pain themselves, or are stretched to their limit. If you put on a wrap soon after an injury, swelling can cause it to become too tight, so check it frequently for the first few hours. Elastic bandages that slip over a joint are also readily available; although you give up the adjustability and versatility of one you wrap yourself, they are very convenient. Watch for swelling below an elastic wrap.

Taping is used where there is a need to take pressure or stress off an affected joint or muscle, for example, after a ligament sprain of the ankle. It is best done by a physical therapist, trainer, or physician, at least initially. You or a friend may be able to copy the taping if taught. Taping is very effective in allowing early mobilization after sprains and helping prevent recurrent injuries, such as ankle sprains.

Preventive Medicine

Prevention is the best medicine. Pay attention to your body. Don't play if you are exhausted, overheated, or dehydrated or if you are experiencing chest pains or shortness of breath. Get in shape, and pay particular attention to your endurance, your muscles, and your flexibility. And finally, warm up and cool down. These principles are truly *first aid*.

Tennis and Total Fitness

15 Nutrition For Tennis and Health

Like all competitive athletes, tennis players are always looking for the little "extra" that will bring them a winning point when it's needed most. Training, technique, strategy, and equipment have been the major tools for sharpening that competitive edge, but in recent years, diet has grown in importance as well.

Medical science still has much to learn about nutrition. Although many uncertainties and controversies exist, we have come a long way in understanding the ideal diet for athletes. A word of caution is in order, however. Nutrition is a highly personal area, and you will encounter many fervent advocates of many different diets. You should beware of fads, extreme diets, and extravagent claims for vitamins or other food additives. This is perhaps the one area in which you should not necessarily emulate world-class players or even your teaching pro. The fact that tournaments have been won by vegetarians, junk food junkies, or megavitamin devotees does not mean that you should follow suit. Instead, you should seek a balanced, reasonable diet that will provide appropriate fuel and fluids for tennis and for daily life.

Over the years tennis players and other athletes have experimented with a great number and variety of dietary regimens designed to improve their performance. The training table is often as heavily laden with lore and superstition as it is with food. In considering nutrition for tennis, it is important to put aside many of these unfounded traditions. In fact, we have now learned that good nutrition for the active athlete is similar to good nutrition for other people. Athletes are nutritionally different from the rest of us only because they require extra calories, extra carbohydrates, and extra water. With this first principle in mind, let's look at the elements of a balanced diet for the tennis player.

189

Calories

In weight-conscious America the calorie has gotten a bad name. In point of fact, the calorie is merely a unit of energy. Each of the foods you eat can be assigned a caloric value, and each of the activities you perform, including tennis, can be measured in terms of the calories you burn up. This simple arithmetic of caloric balance is the single most important determinant of your body weight. If you take in more calories than you burn up, your body will store those extra calories as fat; if you use up more calories than you consume in foods, you will use up fat and lose weight.

Your basic caloric requirements depend on many factors, including your age, sex, size, metabolic rate, and level of activity. In general, men need a few more calories than women, and younger people need more calories than older people to meet basal metabolic needs. The most important variable is exercise, and this is obviously a factor that is also under your own control.

Avid tennis players use more calories. Table 15-1 shows the number of calories that you can expect to burn up in various racquet sports. As you can see, a vigorous game of singles tennis will consume about 500 calories in an hour. If you want to lose weight, this can be helpful; an hour of tennis each day will take off about 1 pound per week. This may not sound like much, but over the course of 6 months or a year the results can really add up. In addition, regular exercise will decrease the percentage of your body weight that is fat and will tone up your muscles so that you will look better. Moreover, exercise may actually suppress your appetite so that you will tend to eat less.

If you want to lose weight, a balanced, calorie-restricted diet is the best way to do so. We strongly advocate a slow, steady approach, with losses of no more than 1 or 2 pounds per week. The problem with most diets is that you lose very quickly at first but regain the weight just as quickly a month or two later. Regular exercise and a balanced diet should enable you to take the weight off and keep it off.

Many tennis players are fit and lean to begin with. If you are lucky enough to belong to this group, you will actually need extra calories to fuel competitive tennis. But don't overdo it. You have to burn 3500 calories to lose 1 pound, so it's a lot easier to put weight on by eating than to take pounds off by playing tennis.

How many calories do you need each day? There are many variables, but you can approximate your caloric needs through

Table 15-1   Caloric cost of racquet sports

Sport	Calories Used per Hour
Badminton (doubles)	240 to 300
Table tennis Badminton (singles) Doubles tennis	300 to 360
Badminton (competitive) Singles tennis	420 to 480
Paddleball Squash	480 to 600
Championship squash	600 to 660

simple arithmetic. If you are sedentary, you will need about 15 calories per pound of body weight per day. If you are very active, you may require twice as many calories. If you are lean and fit, hunger will be the best guide to your daily caloric requirements and you can have the luxury of eating with abandon. If you are fighting the battle of the bulge, calories do count—so you should count them.

Carbohydrates

Carbohydrates have long been unjustly maligned by the diet-conscious public and have even been neglected by some nutritionists. Starchy foods have been labeled fattening and have been rejected as "empty calories." Although it is true that refined sugars and other sweets provide concentrated calories without other nutrients, complex carbohydrates are an excellent source of nutrients. In addition, they are relatively nonfattening: a 6-ounce potato contains only 150 calories, whereas a 6-ounce steak contains 600 calories and potentially harmful fats. Carbohydrates contain just 4 calories per gram, as do proteins. Fats contain more than twice as many calories (9 per gram).

Carbohydrates are organic chemicals containing carbon, hydrogen, and oxygen. The simplest carbohydrate compounds are the sugars; glucose (ordinary sugar) is the body's major carbohydrate energy source. Starches are examples of so-called complex carbohydrates, which are composed of individual sugar molecules attached to each other. All digestible carbohydrates are broken down in your stomach and intestines and are absorbed into the bloodstream as simple sugars, so in the body all carbohydrates are ultimately metabolized as sugar. Refined sugar and other sweets provide concentrated calories without other nutrients, and in this sense they are "empty calories." They can promote tooth decay, but unless you have diabetes or certain other medical problems, refined sugars are not harmful. "Natural" sweets such as honey are no more nutritious than commercially refined sugars, despite a rash of recent promotion.

Even though simple sugars are not harmful, complex carbohydrates are far and away the best source of energy for tennis players. They contain other nutrients besides sugar, they generally add bulk to your diet, and they are absorbed at a more steady and gradual pace than are simple sugars.

Energy for Exercise

Complex carbohydrates are broken down in the intestinal tract into simple carbohydrates and are then absorbed into the bloodstream as glucose (sugar). When you exercise, your muscles need energy, and glucose is the most efficient form of that energy. Blood glucose can be burned for energy or can be stored in your muscles as glycogen. It is actually muscle glycogen that provides the energy you need during tennis. If your muscles run out of glycogen, they will tire out and cramp up. With insufficient carbohydrates in your system, you have to rely on fat or protein for energy. Although fat can be a good source of muscle energy at rest or during quiet activities, it is a poor source of energy during maximal exercise. Fats burn inefficiently and leave toxic residues called ketone bodies, which can impair athletic performance and cause fatigue and dehydration. Proteins are burned for energy only as a last resort when your body is totally depleted of more accessible energy sources such as glycogen and fat.

The average American diet contains only 45% carbohydrates and is unfortunately heavily dependent on refined sugars rather than complex carbohydrates. Carbohydrates should provide 60% to 70% of the caloric content of the athlete's diet.

Because many types of foods are rich in carbohydrates, a high-carbohydrate diet can be nutritionally balanced and can be varied enough to appeal to most players' taste. *Pasta* is an excellent source of carbohydrate, and many enriched spaghetti and noodle products contain important vitamins and minerals as well. *Potatoes* provide iron, vitamins, and fiber, or "roughage," as well as carbohydrates. Obviously baked or boiled potatoes are a much better nutritional "bargain" than fried potatoes, which have additional fat and calories. *Grain products* such as *breads and cereals* are also good sources of carbohydrates. Look for whole-wheat products because they provide needed vitamins and bran (roughage). Avoid sugar-coated cereals. The added sugar will provide calories without nutrients and can promote tooth decay. *Rice* is another good source of carbohydrates, as are *peas and beans,* which also provide protein and minerals. *Fruits and vegetables* supply fiber, vitamins, and minerals in addition to carbohydrates. Moreover, they provide the flavor, variety, and fun that are helpful in maintaining a high-carbohydrate diet. Finally, *skim milk products* are very healthful foods that will give you the carbohydrates you need for tennis while also providing some protein and other nutrients. Yogurt is an excellent example.

Protein

Whereas carbohydrates have been neglected as a source of energy for the athlete, exactly the reverse has been true of protein. Over the years protein has been touted as essential to build muscle strength and endurance in athletes. Steak and eggs have been the mainstay of the training table, and countless thousands of dollars have been spent on protein and amino acid potions for dietary supplements. In fact, this infatuation with protein has extended beyond the athlete to the general public so that steak is the number one prestige food in America, and many weight-reducing diets rely on high-protein foods.

Although it's hard to buck all this traditional teaching, medical evidence has now clearly demonstrated that athletes do not need supplementary protein. The athletic training table should be set with spaghetti or yogurt instead of steak and eggs.

Don't get us wrong—protein is certainly essential for good health. Proteins are high-nitrogen compounds that are composed of individual amino acids linked together. When you eat protein, it is digested in the stomach and intestines and broken down into individual amino acids. The amino acids are then abosrbed and carried in the blood to your tissues, where they are recombined into proteins to provide the structural backbone of your cells.

You need good proteins in your diet to be healthy, but you don't need extra protein to play competitive tennis. Although your muscles are composed principally of proteins, eating extra protein will not build stronger muscles. The only way to increase muscle strength is to exercise regularly and to include enough calories (preferably as carbohydrates) in your diet to give your muscles the energy they need. Moreover, if you attempt to get extra proteins by increasing your proportions of red meat or eggs, you will be getting extra fat in your diet as well, and this may be harmful to your heart and blood vessels.

The protein requirement for the average-size healthy adult is about 50 grams per day. If you are recovering from illness or injury, you may need extra protein. Growing children also need relatively more protein, but for competitive tennis 50 grams per day will do the trick. You don't need to weigh your foods and calculate the amount of protein you eat. If you wish to be precise, simply try to attain 15% of your daily caloric requirement from protein. A sensible, balanced diet should do the trick. Above all, don't waste your money on the commerical potions, pills, or powders containing extra protein or amino acids; a healthful diet will provide all the protein you need at much less expense.

Red meats are an excellent source of high-quality protein, but they are also high in fats; as a result, they have more calories and may contribute to elevated cholesterol levels. This does not mean that you have to abandon all red meat. However, current evidence suggests that you may help your heart without harming your ability to play tennis by substituting less fatty sources of protein whenever possible. Poultry, fish, skim milk products, and legumes such as soybeans are the most healthful sources of proteins.

Fat

Although tennis players and their coaches often argue about carbohydrate and protein in their diets, it is the doctors and nutritionists who argue about the potential risks of dietary fats. There is in fact some uncertainty about the role of high-fat intake in producing heart disease. However, the bulk of the evidence suggests that such a link does exist. Without going into the scientific details, we would like to pass along the general dietary recommendations endorsed by the American Heart Association and other organizations.

The average American diet contains more than 40% of its calories in fat. Fat is very high in calories, containing 9 calories per gram, which is more than twice the amount found in carbohydrates or proteins. Tennis players should get no more than 25% of their daily calories from fat. In addition, it is important to choose carefully the type of fat you eat.

Animal fats, such as those found in meat and eggs, are saturated fats and are high in cholesterol. These are the fats which contribute to atherosclerosis and heart disease. In contrast, vegetable fats are generally unsaturated and much more healthful.

Try to limit your intake of saturated fats to no more than 50% of your total fat intake. This means reducing the amount of red meat, egg yolks, butter, cream, ice cream, and whole milk. You don't have to avoid all meats, but try to choose leaner cuts and be certain to trim the fat and bake or broil your meat instead of frying. Vegetable oil such as safflower, soybean, or corn oils will give you an excellent source of unsaturated fats. Skim milk products will provide protein and calcium without saturated fat.

There is no evidence that modifying your fat intake will in any way help your tennis game. There is good evidence that it will help your heart, however, and that certainly warrants some effort in changing your dietary habits.

Dietary Fiber

High-fiber diets are now the rage. Although we have been skeptical of many other diet fads, there is good medical evidence that a high-fiber diet *is* healthful. Fiber, or roughage, in your diet will facilitate the emptying of your colon. This prevents constipation and decreases the likelihood of diseases of the colon such as diverticulosis. There is even some evidence that a high-fiber diet may decrease the risk of colon cancer, gallstones, hemorrhoids, and other conditions. More scientific study is needed of these possible benefits.

Fiber is the portion of food that cannot be digested and which therefore enters the colon intact, pulling along water so that the stools are bulkier and softer. Dietary fiber is found in raw unskinned fruits, root vegetables, and especially in whole grain or bran.

High-fiber diets will help your digestion and your health. However, a word of caution is in order for tennis players. In some people, high-roughage diets can produce gas and bloating. You may even develop some abdominal cramps until you get used to this diet. Obviously, a bloated belly will slow down your tennis game. To avoid this, try to increase the amount of fiber in your diet slowly, and if you are subject to bloating, avoid high-fiber foods on the day of a big match.

Vitamins

Vitamins are probably the most controversial aspect of the athlete's diet. Many winning tennis players swear by megavitamins. Other vitamin advocates are quick to recommend vitamin supplements for everything from the common cold to sexual impotence. It would certainly be nice if you could improve your tennis, your health, and your sex life with a few vitamin pills. Unfortunately, scientific evidence suggests that these claims are nothing more than wishful thinking.

Make no mistake about the fact that vitamins are essential for your health. Vitamins are organic chemicals that your body cannot make for itself which are indispensable for your metabolism. The question is not whether you need vitamins (you do), but whether you need supplementary vitamins in pill form. The best scientific evidence suggests that a well-balanced diet should provide all the vitamins you need.

There are basically two types of vitamins: vitamins A, D, E, and K are *fat-soluble vitamins*. They are eaten with fat-containing foods and are absorbed into body along with fat. In your body they are stored in your organs. Very large reserves of the fat-soluble vitamins can be stored in this way so that you do not need to eat foods containing these vitamins each day. However, because of this storage, excessive intake of these vitamins can lead to toxic levels. In particular, excessive dosages of vitamins A or D can produce serious side effects.

In contrast, the eight B vitamins and vitamin C are *water-soluble vitamins*. They are not stored by your body to any appreciable degree, so you do need to take in these vitamins at frequent (if not daily) intervals. Because water-soluble vitamins are not stored in your body, moderate supplementary doses are safe. However, if the dose you take in exceeds the amount your body needs, the excess will simply be spilled in your urine without providing any health benefits whatsoever. Because vitamins are needed in such tiny amounts, a well-balanced diet should provide all you need.

As physicians, we do sometimes prescribe vitamins. Pregnant and lactating women certainly need vitamins. Elderly people, malnourished individuals, alcoholics, and food faddists all benefit from vitamins. For a healthy tennis player, however, a well-balanced diet will suffice.

In general, vitamin pills are not harmful. Very high doses of vitamins A and D can produce serious side effects, and excessive doses of vitamin C can sometimes produce kidney stones. The doses contained in the average multivitamin pill are really quite safe. If you feel healthier and more self-confident as a result of taking multivitamins, go right ahead. This sense of confidence may even help you on the tennis court. Choose the least expensive preparation that satisfies your needs; remember that "natural" vitamins are no better than synthetic vitamins. But don't be pulled into a false sense of security: vitamin supplements do not automatically ensure good nutrition. Your body requires a balanced intake of carbohydrates, fat, protein, water, and minerals in addition to vitamins.

Water

The most important nutrient that you need during a hard tennis match is also the simplest and the most neglected element of the athlete's diet: water.

You definitely need extra fluids to sustain long tennis matches. You can prove this to yourself by weighing yourself before and after playing. Each pound that you lose during a tennis match represents a pint of water, which must be replaced. The amount of fluids you can lose are truly astounding, especially if you are playing in hot, humid weather.

Exercise generates a tremendous amount of body heat. To dissipate the heat, the body must sweat. In muggy weather you can lose more than 2 quarts of water in just 1 hour of hard tennis. Even in cooler weather you lose substantial amounts of fluids. Dehydration will definitely hurt your tennis game by producing fatigue, muscle cramps, and even mental depression, which can dull your competitive edge. If losing a match isn't bad enough, dehydration can also sometimes contribute to serious medical illness such as heat exhaustion, heat stroke, and kidney damage.

To prevent these problems, you should drink before, during, and after each tennis match. The amount you need will depend on how hard you are playing and on the weather. In warm weather we suggest taking 6 to 8 ounces before you start playing and an additional 4 to 6 ounces during each changeover. The sensation of thirst lags behind your body's need for fluids, so you can't rely on thirst alone to guide you. Even if you don't feel thirsty at the end of your match, be sure to drink plenty.

The fluid we prefer is cool water. The commercially available athletic replacement solutions such as Gatorade and ERG contain sugar, salt, and potassium, which aren't necessary during exercise and in rare cases may even be harmful. Still, the type of fluid is actually less important than the amount of fluid you drink. An ounce of prevention, in this case, may require a quart of water. Drink early and often.

Minerals

Minerals are important in the diet of every tennis player, but like vitamins, supplementary minerals are not required if you eat a well-balanced diet. At least 15 mineral elements are required in trace amounts to maintain health, three of which merit special discussion.

Salt (sodium) has been added to the athlete's diet for years, often in the form of salt tablets. However, extra salt is not necessary for the tennis player—in fact, it can even be harmful. Although sodium is lost in sweat, a normal diet provides more than enough to replace the amount you lose, even in summer tennis. When you sweat, you lose more water than salt so that your blood salt concentration may actually rise temporarily. This is why water is the ideal replacement fluid during exercise.

High-salt diets may contribute to high blood pressure (hypertension). The average American diet contains much more salt than we need, which may be one reason why 15% of all American adults have hypertension. Because of this, we advise you to limit the amount of salt you eat. This means cutting back on fast foods, processed foods, and junk foods. You should even try to use less salt in cooking and at the table. If you play lots of tennis in hot weather, you may want to add a little table salt. If your normal diet is very low in salt and you sweat a great deal, you can take a cup of bouillon for each 2 quarts you sweat (5 pounds weight loss). This should give you all the sodium you need, so salt tablets are almost never required by the athlete.

Potassium is also provided in sufficient quantity in a normal diet. Orange juice and bananas are especially high in potassium. Although potassium is lost in sweat, your diet should give you plenty without the need for supplements. In fact, your blood potassium level may actually rise during exercise because potassium is stored in your muscle cells, and when your muscles work hard, they may release potassium to your bloodstream. This is another reason we prefer water to high–sugar-salt-potassium solutions as replacement fluids during exercise.

Iron is another mineral that is lost in sweat but not in large enough amounts to require supplementation. Iron is the single mineral that does often require supplementation, particularly in women. Red meat is the best dietary source of iron. Since many tennis players are turning away from high-meat diets, they will have to get their iron from deep green vegetables (beet greens, spinach, and kale), raisins, and especially enriched or fortified breads and cereals. If women tennis players eat enough of these high-iron foods, they should not need supplements. Because iron is lost during each menstrual period, iron deficiency anemia can develop. Have your red blood cell level tested during each medical checkup; if you are anemic, your doctor may prescribe iron supplements.

The Pregame Meal

An area of great interest to the tennis player is the pregame meal. Although some athletes, such as marathon runners, undergo elaborate carbohydrate depletion and loading diets during the week before a race, this is not necessary for tennis, since even a five-set match is not likely to deplete your muscle glycogen reserves. However, it is important to continue a high-carbohydrate diet in the days before a big match.

The most important advice about the pregame meal is to skip it. A large meal will divert blood from your muscles to your intestines and can definitely impair your game. You should eat little or nothing for about 2 hours before you play, although you should drink water during this period. What you eat 3 or more hours before playing depends on personal experience and preference. In general, we recommend a light meal of high-carbohydrate foods, such as yogurt. Avoid high-fiber foods, which may cause gas and bloating. Similarly, spicy or heavy foods can cause indigestion, and high-fat foods may also produce digestive symptoms and sluggishness.

Sugar, candy, or honey, unfortunately, do not provide extra energy before or during your match. In fact, concentrated sugar may actually harm your performance. There are two reasons for this. First, extra fluids are retained in your stomach and intestines when you eat sugar. This fluid retention may cause bloating and can delay the absorption of fluid into your bloodstream, where it is needed. Second, your body responds to the extra sugar by secreting the hormone insulin. High blood insulin levels may temporarily impede the ability of your muscles to use glycogen for energy. As a result, sugar may actually give you less energy if you eat it just before or during a match. Instead, you should rely on a high-carbohydrate diet in the days before a tournament rather than attempting a "quick fix" with sugar at the time of the match itself.

Caffeine and Alcohol

In addition to a candy bar, two other items that some tennis players favor are caffeine and alcohol. Alcohol can impair concentration and coordination and should be avoided before playing. However, modest amounts of alcohol are not harmful to healthy people. On the contrary, some recent studies suggest that up to two drinks per day may actually lessen the likelihood of heart attacks. We are not prescribing alcohol, but there is no reason to abstain from moderate amounts of beer, wine, or alcohol to toast your victories or to soften your defeats—after the game. The key is moderation.

Caffeine is also a highly personal and somewhat controversial area. Some evidence suggests that coffee may help delay muscle glycogen depletion, but it does not seem likely that this will improve your tennis. There is some concern that caffeine may contribute to a variety of diseases ranging from fibrocystic disease of the breast to cancer of the pancreas. Medical evidence for these worries is still preliminary and fragmentary, so it is too early to advise you to avoid coffee on medical grounds. Caffeine may make you tense or jittery, and in some people caffeine can produce palpitations (rapid heartbeat). Any of these side effects will surely interfere with top-flight tennis. In the last analysis the amount of caffeine you take is up to you. If it seems to perk you up, you can indulge, but if you get a pounding heart or shaking hand, avoid it. Remember that, although coffee is the most well-known caffeine source, tea, cola drinks, and cocoa also contain substantial amounts.

● ● ●

Your diet by itself cannot bring you victory on the court. Still, a balanced diet containing lots of carbohydrates, appropriate nutrients, the right number of calories, and plentiful fluids will contribute to winning tennis and to good health.

16   Tennis and Your Heart

In Chapter 1 of *Tennis Medic* we examined conditioning for tennis, exploring ways to get your body into shape to play your best. In this last chapter we look at the other side of the coin: how can tennis contribute to your total fitness and overall health? It will not surprise you to learn that the heart of the matter is, in fact, your heart.

The Normal Heart and Circulation

As athletes, we spend a great deal of time thinking about our muscles, both in planning ways to strengthen them and in wondering why they are subject to stiffness, aches, and other malfunctions at various times. However, we spend comparatively little time thinking about the body's most important muscle, the heart. Fortunately, the heart muscle does not require any thought to keep it working because its functions are entirely automatic. Still, a little thought about your life-style can go a long way to keeping your heart healthy.

The heart is a muscle whose job is to pump blood throughout the body. Blood from all the body's tissues is collected into blood vessels called veins that finally empty into the heart. From there, the blood is pumped into the lungs. In the lungs, carbon dioxide, a waste product of tissue metabolism, passes out from the blood into the air. At the same time the oxygen that is required to nourish all tissues enters the blood. The oxygen-rich blood now returns to the heart and is finally pumped out to the body's tissues.

This may seem complicated, rather dull, and a long way from center court, but don't close the book just yet—there are three practical consequences of this anatomy and physiology.

The first point is that, as a muscle, the heart needs its own arteries to provide it with oxygen and nutrients. The job of carrying oxygen to the heart falls to the coronary arteries, which are small vessels with big jobs: if the flow of blood to the heart is interrupted, illness or death will result. Indeed, coronary artery disease is the number one killer in the United States, being responsible for angina pectoris, heart attacks, congestive heart failure, and sudden death from disorders of the heart's pumping rhythm.

Second, for the heart to pump blood to the whole body, it must generate a substantial amount of pressure. The exact magnitude of this pressure is measured quite accurately each time your blood pressure is checked. High blood pressure, or hypertension, means extra work for your heart and your arteries. Hypertension rivals coronary artery disease as a crucial health problem in the United States today.

A third important point about normal cardiac function is that the heart does not work alone but is intimately linked to the lungs and blood vessels. The lungs work like bellows to bring oxygen to the blood and remove carbon dioxide. The blood vessels are a vast network of canals for the distribution of oxygen to and removal of wastes from tissues. Among these tissues are the muscles that work so hard when you play tennis. The oxygen demands of of exercising muscles are truly extraordinary, exceeding their resting requirements by tenfold or more. Thus exercise produces a complex set of demands on your lungs, heart, circulation, and muscles all at once. This is the true meaning of total fitness: in addition to preventing the diseases that can cripple any part of this complex network, we must seek ways to enhance the capacities of even healthy organ systems to provide for optimal body function.

Diseases of the Heart and Circulation

In contemporary American society cardiovascular disease is almost epidemic. In 1980, for example, there were nearly 1 million deaths in our country from cardiovascular disease. This staggering figure accounts for nearly half of all the deaths reported in the United States, making cardiovascular disease our number one killer.

Looked at another way, these statistics reveal that Americans suffer approximately two heart attacks during each and every minute of the year. Why is the incidence of cardiac disease so high? More important, is there anything we can do to stem the tide?

Although all the answers are not yet in, medical science is making great strides in understanding the causes of coronary artery disease and in devising strategies to help prevent this problem. Even tennis may have some role in protecting you.

Risk Factors

There are various conditions that can put you in greater jeopardy of developing coronary heart disease. Some of these so-called risk factors are beyond our control, whereas others may be subject to modification by you and your doctor. Risk factors that are beyond your control include *male sex* and *heredity*; men are at much higher risk of heart disease than women, and if your family history includes many cases of heart disease, you are at greater risk than you would be if your family tree were notable for longevity instead. Another major risk factor that can be inherited is *diabetes*; you can control diabetes with diet, exercise, and medication, but you still run an increased risk of getting cardiovascular disease.

Smoking. You cannot trade in your grandparents, but you can do a lot to modify some of the other risk factors. Smoking is a major contributor to heart disease. You are all aware of the damage smoking can do to your lungs, ranging from emphysema to lung cancer, and you probably know that smoking is a major cause of oral and laryngeal cancer. Yet many people are not aware of the important ways in which cigarette smoking damages blood vessels, including the coronary arteries. There can no longer be any doubt that cigarette smoking is a major hazard to health, causing disease, disability, and death from both heart and lung diseases.

As a tennis player, you should be motivated to abstain from smoking because of the immediate effects of cigarettes on your endurance, or "wind." In a sense, then, tennis and other sports may help reduce this risk factor by providing motivation in terms of immediate rewards that are easy to see and feel. If you need more motivation, just remember that, for each cigarette you smoke, your life expectancy decreases. Only you can decide to quit. You can get help in the form of support groups, behavior modification techniques, and even hypnosis. Clearly, this is not a question for your tennis pro (unless he's a reformed smoker) but for your physician. The local chapters of the Lung Association and the American Cancer Society are also excellent sources of information on how to stop smoking.

Hypertension. Another major risk factor that requires medical help to recognize and treat is hypertension, or high blood pressure. Hypertension is one of the most common chronic diseases in America, affecting an estimated 23 million people, or 1 out of every 7 adults.

The causes of hypertension are numerous and complex. In fact, despite extensive study, the root cause of hypertension is unknown in the majority of cases, which are therefore diagnosed as "essential" hypertension. We do know that excess salt intake can contribute to hypertension (Chapter 15). We also know that effective treatment is available for almost all patients and that the damaging effects of high blood pressure can be prevented by such treatment.

Elevated blood pressure puts excessive demands on your heart and blood vessels. The damage that results can produce heart attacks, heart failure, stroke, or kidney disease. The trick is to detect hypertension before damage occurs. Do not count on nosebleeds, headaches, flushing, or tension as warnings. In most cases high blood pressure is present for years before producing any symptoms. Clearly, the name "silent killer" is well earned.Even tournament-level players may have undetected hypertension. The only way to be certain is to have your blood pressure checked.

There are several steps you can take to help prevent hypertension and to treat mild or moderate elevations of your blood pressure. Salt restriction, weight reduction, and relaxation are examples. In many cases medications are also required, so you will need your physician's help. Don't stay away from your doctor for fear of being taken off the courts because of hypertension; in fact, your doctor may prescribe more tennis, since regular exercise can be an important element in blood pressure control.

Stress. Two other risk factors are worthy of mention, although they seem less important than the factors just discussed. One is life stress and personality type. It does seem that the so-called type-A or coronary-prone personality is indeed at greater risk for heart disease. This set of personal characteristics is best summarized by another medical synonym, "hurry sickness." Among the features of the type-A style are rushing, doing two or three things at once, feeling time pressure and constantly referring to clocks, and being unable to relax, which often leads to a preference for work over leisure. Although this life-style is bad for the heart, type-A individuals are competitive and often highly successful in many walks of life—including tennis! But this sort of success may not be worth the price you may pay. The effects on stress of exercise in general and tennis in particular are assessed later in this chapter.

Obesity and cholesterol. Obesity is a potential risk factor that can be helped by exercise. Note that we have qualified obesity as a "potential" risk factor only. Although obese people do have more heart attacks than thin people, the difference is probably not in obesity per se but is accounted for by the other adverse factors associated with obesity such as diabetes, high blood pressure, and high cholesterol.

High cholesterol is the most widely publicized risk factor, and there can be no doubt that elevations of your blood cholesterol level increase your risk of having a heart attack. However, it is a bit more complex. There are two different types of cholesterol. The "bad" cholesterol, which can clog coronary arteries and thus cause heart attacks, is the so-called low-density lipoprotein (LDL) cholesterol. Another type of cholesterol may actually help protect against coronary artery disease; this is the so-called high-density lipoprotein (HDL) cholesterol.

The only way you will know if you have an elevated cholesterol level is to have it checked by a blood test. A variety of medications can be used to lower cholesterol, but you are much better off if you can help yourself by life-style modification instead. In the preceding chapter we examined the impact of diet and weight on cholesterol. Another way to favorably influence your blood fats is through exercise, including tennis.

Physical inactivity. There is no doubt that a lack of exercise and a sedentary life-style can contribute to heart disease, and some interesting studies of exercise and health are summarized later. Despite all this evidence, however, some members of the medical community have been a bit slow to recognize the importance of exercise. Perhaps this is because many doctors are themselves overworked and sedentary, or perhaps it is because the treatment lies with the public rather than the physician. It is true that the final proof is not yet in, but even the conservative medical establishment now generally accepts the health benefits of exercise. As tennis players, we are sure you will, too.

Exercise and Your Heart

How often have you been advised to "take it easy—you'll live longer"? This is one of the few situations in which folk wisdom has proved to be incorrect. Hopefully, our children will be encouraged instead to "get off your duff—you'll live longer."

Types of Exercise: Isometric Versus Isotonic

Exercise can contribute to health, but not all forms of exercise are equally beneficial. In isometric exercise, such as weight lifting, muscles work hard against resistance; they shorten little but generate lots of tension. Muscular strength improves, but isometrics raise the blood pressure and heart rate substantially and can stress the heart without building aerobic power. In contrast, isotonic work allows muscles to work through a greater range of motion against less resistance; as a result, muscles shorten more but generate less tension. Examples of isotonic exercise include walking, running, swimming, rowing, and, yes, tennis itself. Isotonic exercise forces your heart to work hard also, but it pumps greater volumes of blood against lower resistance or pressure, and this type of work load seems quite beneficial.

Benefits of Exercise: Risk Factor Modifications

Tennis and other forms of endurance exercise can do a lot for your health. Many of the risk factors that contribute to coronary heart disease can be modified favorably by endurance exercise.

Blood pressure tends to be lower in conditioned athletes, both at rest and during exercise. In fact, aerobic training is itself a good form of treatment for mild to moderate hypertension. We always encourage our hypertensive patients to try life-style modification before resorting to medication. Exercise, salt restriction, weight reduction, and stress control constitute this first line of treatment. Not all people with high blood pressure can be fully controlled in these ways, but even if medications are needed to normalize their blood pressure, they will probably require lower doses and fewer drugs if they are physically fit.

Body composition and blood fats are also improved by regular aerobic exercise. The percentage of your body that is fat will decrease as you get into shape. You will see the rewards in your appearance, and you will feel the benefits on the tennis court. However, the changes that you cannot see may ultimately be the most beneficial. Exercise tends to decrease the total cholesterol level, a desirable effect. Even more striking is the way in which endurance exercise affects the HDL cholesterol. Remember that this is the "good" cholesterol; the higher your levels, the lower is your risk of arteriosclerosis. A recent study from Stanford University showed that tennis players have higher levels of HDL cholesterol than do sedentary people. In men the levels were 57.8 in players and 46.2 in nonplayers, whereas women players had very high levels of 73.9 compared with 61.7 in nonplayers. These potentially helpful changes were independent of diet, alcohol consumption, and smoking.

Endurance exercise affects many additional metabolic functions of your body. For example, the body's tissues become more sensitive to the effects of the hormone insulin, so glucose (sugar) utilization improves. In fact, exercise is one of the oldest forms of treatment for diabetes. Even in this era of medical sophistication and space age technology, some of these venerable clinical observations deserve rediscovery. If you have diabetes, we cannot promise that you will be able to cast off your insulin needles in favor of tennis shoes—but the chances are excellent that your requirements for medication will decrease. Many of our patients have been able to discontinue their medication altogether.

These physiologic and biochemical effects of exercise are relatively easy to study and to quantitate with laboratory tests. The *psychologic effects of exercise* are much harder to pinpoint, but they are no less real and important. Just think of how you feel after a hard workout: tired, yes, but also relaxed and (barring a close defeat in a five-set tournament final) exhilarated simultaneously. Endurance exercise may not be a "natural high," but it is beneficial psychologically. All in all, the psychologic effects of exercise may help prevent heart disease indirectly by reducing stress and by encouraging behavior modification in terms of what you eat, what you drink, and what you smoke.

Exercise and Longevity

Lower blood pressure, lower total cholesterol with increased HDL cholesterol, less body fat, lower body weight, better blood sugar levels, and stress reduction—it sounds great. But what is the evidence that exercise actually prevents heart attacks and prolongs life?

Over the past 20 years there have been numerous investigations of the effects of exercise on heart disease and longevity. To shed light on this question, large numbers of people must be observed over a period of many years. As a result, these studies are quite difficult to perform, and their conclusions tend to vary in many details. Even so, one consistent theme has emerged from the majority of these investigations: exercise does indeed prolong life by reducing cardiac disease.

Unfortunately, no one has yet investigated the longevity of tennis players themselves, but the potential benefits of tennis can be inferred from other studies. Dr. Ralph Paffenbarger and his colleagues at Stanford University conducted a very interesting evaluation of 16,936 Harvard alumni who entered college between 1916 and 1950. All in all, there were 117,680 man-years of observation. Their results are striking. High activity levels reduced the risk of heart attack by

Table 16-1   The time required to perform 2000 Kcal of exercise

Sport	Length of Exercise (Hours)
Ballet	7
Bicycling (10 miles/hour)	5
Bowling	8
Brisk walking	5
Calisthenics	7
Doubles tennis	7
Golf	8
Jogging (6 miles/hour)	3
Singles tennis	4¾
Squash, racquetball	4

an impressive 26%, and this protection was valid for all age groups between 35 and 74. The Stanford investigation also found that, although even low levels of exercise are of some help, a total energy expenditure of 2000 Kcal per week provides optimal benefit. This information can facilitate planning an effective exercise schedule.

Another observation from this study is of interest. The benefits of exercise apply only if you keep on exercising: even those who were varsity competitors during their undergraduate years were no better off than their sedentary classmates unless they continued to exercise. The converse was also found to be true: men who took up active life-styles later in life still got the benefits of exercise.

Obviously there are many ways to get in your weekly 2000 Kcal of exercise. Paffenbarger found that active sports were somewhat more beneficial than less strenuous activities such as walking and stair climbing, but there is nothing to suggest that one sport is better for you than another. The bottom line is the intensity, duration, and frequency of exercise.

How does tennis stack up? Table 16-1 compares the approximate amount of time you need to put in each week to reach the 2000 Kcal level through tennis and other sports. As you can see, tennis is not the most efficient sport in terms of energy expenditure per hour. Still, since you are exercising for enjoyment as well as for health, and since tennis is your favorite game, it can be the core of your exercise program. In terms of what tennis can do for your health, tennis *could* be your only form of exercise, but in terms of what you can do for your tennis, other conditioning activities are useful in a balanced fitness program. Part I of *Tennis Medic* presents a balanced exercise program for tennis.

Heart Disease Prevention

If you are exercising regularly in the 2000 Kcal per week range, you are to be congratulated for not resting in your sneakers—but don't rest on your laurels either. There are other important steps you can take to prevent heart disease. An earlier Paffenbarger study, in which 3686 San Francisco longshoremen were observed for 22 years, illustrates some of these factors. Exercise was the single most important variable in predicting the risk of heart attacks: physically active longshoremen had 50% fewer heart attacks than did otherwise similar longshoremen with more sedentary jobs. This study looked at other variables as well: nonsmokers had 30% less heart disease than smokers, and men with normal blood pressure were 30% less likely to suffer heart attacks than were hypertensive subjects. Paffenbarger estimated that all three interventions (exercise, cessation of smoking, and control of hypertension) could collectively reduce heart attacks by 88%. We would add good nutrition and weight control to this list, as discussed in Chapter 15.

We are already seeing the benefits of these life-style changes. Between 1968 and 1976 there has been a 20% decrease in heart disease in the United States. We have a long way to go, but our efforts are starting to pay off.

Tennis and Aging

Perhaps the best way to summarize these effects is to look at exercise and aging. The aging process is gradual, continuous, and inevitable. We have much to learn about aging, but certain changes have been reasonably well defined. All the organs of your body are involved. Muscular strength declines, and the flexibility of ligaments and joints decreases. Whereas muscle mass diminishes, the percentage of your body composition that is fat increases. Bones may lose calcium and therefore have less strength and resistance to stress. The nervous system also is affected by age: reaction time increases so that your reflexes are slower. In addition, the heart and circulation show the effects of time. Your heart's maximum ability to pump blood decreases, and in some cases blood vessels narrow as a result of fatty deposits (atherosclerosis). Blood pressure tends to increase with age. Not surprisingly, your lungs also change over the years. The lung capacity decreases, and the chest wall becomes stiffer so that oxygen delivery declines. The net effect of these changes is that your body's capacity to perform work diminishes as you age. As a rough estimate, work capacity declines by about 50% over the 50 years between ages 25 and 75.

The good news is that you can modify almost all these aging processes in a favorable direction. The answer is not the fountain of youth, but regular exercise. You should be sure to include two very important elements in your exercise program. The first is endurance training, or aerobics. This will tend to increase heart and lung capacities, lower blood pressure, and lower body fat. In fact, endurance training will even improve reaction time both on and off the court. As discussed earlier in this chapter and in Chapter 1, tennis itself is a good endurance activity. Because flexibility decreases with age, injuries become a greater risk each year. So the second component of your fitness program should be a series of exercises for flexibility and strength. These elements of your fitness program are outlined in Chapters 2 and 3.

You can continue playing tennis into your "senior citizen" years. For years spectators have marveled at the skills and stamina displayed at masters tournaments. Now Ken Rosewall, Billie Jean King, and other top stars are performing on professional tours, which should inspire fans of all ages. These players are "old" only in comparison with the high-school wonders who are starting to dominate tournament play, particularly on the women's circuit. We are even more impressed with the super-seniors—players older than 55 who play excellent competitive tennis.

Clarence Chaffee is a case in point. Chaffee was the tennis and squash coach at Williams College for 33 years but did not begin competing nationally until age 70. Since then he has collected 41 national super-seniors titles. Tennis will not make you immune from heart disease, and even the remarkable Mr. Chaffee demonstrates this point: he had a heart attack at age 82. But 5 months (and one pacemaker) later he was back on the courts, and so far he's won seven more national titles in his age group.

Our thesis is simple: exercise is good for your tennis, and tennis is one of the exercises that is good for your heart and your health. Our enthusiasm for exercise stops short of fanaticism, and we must admit that exercise has its limitations and even its hazards. Everybody can exercise, but you must be certain that your program is suitable for your level of health. Medical checkups are important to evaluate your ability to play competitive tennis. The musculoskeletal hazards of tennis are covered in Part II of this book. Let's consider now the potential cardiac hazards of tennis and some other forms of exercise.

Tennis and Your Heart: Potential Pitfalls and Precautions

Despite the claims of a few physicians, even the most comprehensive programs of exercise and diet cannot confer immunity to coronary artery disease and heart attacks. All tennis players know that Arthur Ashe is a prime example of the "exception that proves the rule." Ashe is an active, thin nonsmoker who had a heart attack in 1979, ultimately leading to coronary artery bypass surgery. He had an excellent recovery, only to require a second operation 4 years later. His case does not disprove the value of tennis and other forms of exercise; in fact, both Ashe and his doctors believe that his recovery has been aided by his excellent physical condition. It does remind us that prudence and medical guidance are essential in certain situations.

Tennis itself cannot harm your heart, but if you have underlying heart disease from other causes, strenuous exercise can surely precipitate serious problems. Until fairly recently many doctors believed that exercise actually caused heart trouble. Some patients were even given the diagnosis of "athlete's heart." It is true that athletes tend to have lower blood pressure and strikingly slower heart rates. Careful physical and x-ray examinations may reveal enlargement of the heart, and electrocardiograms may reflect similar changes. These "abnormalities" are not a disease; in fact, we now know that the athlete's heart is a healthy heart with a strong, efficient pumping mechanism.

Death During Sports

Even though deaths on the tennis court are very rare, they merit careful consideration so that we can do everything possible to prevent them. First, not all of the sudden deaths in athletes are due to cardiac causes. Drug abuse, heat stroke, and even severe allergic reactions to insect stings can be just as lethal. In other cases ruptured blood vessels can mimic cardiac death.

Bona fide cardiac deaths that do occur in athletes fall into two general groups. In younger individuals the leading causes are congenital, or inborn, abnormalities. In older people ordinary coronary heart disease is usually to blame. Sudden exertion increases the heart's demand for blood, but if the coronary arteries have blockages, oxygen delivery is impaired and muscle damage or disorders of the heart's pumping rhythm can result.

The best way to prevent major cardiac problems on the court is to detect latent abnormalities before they cause illness. This will require cooperation between you and your doctor. Your job is to reduce risk factors and to report early symptoms. Your doctor's job is to perform appropriate medical examinations and screening tests.

Warning Signs and Medical Tests

Although heart disease can be silent, you should be familiar with certain warning symptoms. Chest pain is the most obvious distress signal. Heart pain typically causes a dull, heavy pressure in the midchest. The pain may radiate to the neck, jaw, or arms. It is usually brought on by exertion or emotion and is relieved by rest or by certain medications such as nitroglycerin. However, cardiac pain may be seen in many disguises and may even be confused with indigestion. Other symptoms that warrant medical evaluation include undue fatigue or shortness of breath, unexpected nausea, sweating or lightheadedness, and a sensation of erratic heart rhythm or skipped beats.

Any of these symptoms should prompt you to get a checkup, and even young, apparently healthy players should have a periodic medical evaluation. At the minimum, this should include a review of your medical history and current symptoms, as well as a physical examination. A blood count and urinalysis are often included in the initial evaluation of young athletes. However, more detailed studies should be done if you have any of the symptoms just listed or if you have any cardiac risk factors, such as a positive family history, hypertension, smoking, diabetes, or obesity. Finally, if you are just starting to get into shape after being sedentary, or if you are older than 40, more detailed studies are probably indicated.

These studies might include blood chemistry tests such as kidney function tests and fasting blood sugar and cholesterol determinations. A chest x-ray examination can screen for lung disease and enlargement of the heart, but because this involves exposure to radiation, it should not be done indiscriminately or repeated unnecessarily.

The electrocardiogram (ECG) is another important screening test. Although ECGs are not needed for healthy young adults, they can be helpful for older tennis players. The ordinary ECG may be perfectly normal in many people with heart disease, so your physician may order an exercise test if you have worrisome symptoms or if you belong to any of the increased risk categories cited previously. In this test you will be asked to exercise on a treadmill or bike while your ECG is recorded continuously and your blood pressure is checked periodically. The physical exertion duplicates or exceeds the stress of tennis and will hopefully allow your doctor to detect abnormalities in the heart's blood supply, pumping rhythm, or blood pressure under carefully controlled circumstances.

Practical Precautions

Not even the stress test is infallible, and it can never replace common sense on the court as a safety factor. What simple precautions should you take?

First, never attempt to play all-out after a period of inactivity, especially if it is due to illness. Get your heart and circulation in shape with aerobic conditioning, and get your muscles and joints ready with stretching and calisthenics before you resume competitive play. Your first few times out should be half-speed workouts. In particular, if you have a viral illness with fever and muscle ache, you should refrain from strenuous play; there is some experimental evidence that exercise may predispose you to viral inflammation of the heart if you overexert yourself with a virus in your system.

Second, remember to warm up gradually before each match and to cool down slowly afterward. Your heart is most vulnerable when it is subjected to abrupt changes, so give it a chance to get into gear. Stretching exercises, calisthenics, and jogging can be very useful in the warm-up and cool-down because they will help prevent muscular injuries while they protect your heart from sudden stress.

Third, modify your game to fit prevailing conditions. These conditions can be external or internal. For example, hot weather calls for less strenuous play and for copious fluid replacement. Similarly, if you are feeling below par, don't push yourself to the limit—a tennis match just is not important enough for you to jeopardize your health.

The fourth and most important piece of advice is very simple but often overlooked: listen to your body. It is surprisingly easy to deny warning symptoms in the heat of competition. Don't do it. If you feel unwell, retire from your game; if your symptoms are severe or persistent, get medical attention promptly.

"Cardiac Tennis"

One of the most common reasons that tennis players avoid doctors is that they are afraid they will be taken off the courts if a heart problem is detected. But people with heart disease can continue playing tennis with qualifications. Obviously each case must be evaluated individually by a physician with a good understanding of heart disease and exercise physiology. Each patient requires expert stress testing and an individual exercise prescription. In general, people with hypertension or even mild stable angina pectoris can play with few restrictions if they are receiving medication, are free of symptoms, and have favorable exercise tests. Similarly, most patients with pacemakers can return to the courts if they are free of other problems. Patients with more serious problems require supervision and special precautions.

Many hospitals around the country offer cardiac rehabilitation programs, which provide supervised exercise regimens for patients with heart disease. At the Massachusetts General Hospital Cardiovascular Health Center, the majority of our patients have suffered heart attacks, undergone coronary artery bypass surgery, or both. We have had great success in helping these patients return to an active life. Our major training tools are walking, jogging, and riding a stationary bike. Often tennis buffs are eager to return to play, and graded exercise training under careful medical supervision will generally permit them to play tennis. We have had the opportunity to monitor our patients' heart rate during tennis through the use of telemetric ECG recordings. The highest heart rates occur during service, rushing the net, or tense competition. In some cases peak heart rates at these times exceed what is safe for our patients, but we do not take these patients off the court. Instead, we modify the rules. If you see a game of ''two-bounce tennis,'' a three-player match, or a game in which no net play is allowed, you may be seeing ''cardiac tennis.'' We also condition our patients to take a loss with a smile. This is actually easier than you might think. Just playing at all is enough to bring a smile to their faces, and even cardiac tennis requires great skill and produces good fun.

●　●　●

In the last few pages we have focused on a minority of the millions of tennis players in the country. Although common sense and medical screening are important for everyone, most of us can play with abandon and actually improve our health in the process. Yet we urge a final cardiac precaution for even the healthiest tournament player: learn cardiopulmonary resuscitation. The American Red Cross offers cardiopulmonary resuscitation courses at convenient times and places all over the United States. In just three sessions you can learn simple techniques that can save a life on or off the court. The life you save may be . . . your partner's.

Index